The Journey

Hearing from God and learning from each other

Lianne Semans Smith & Lee Herdman

Scripture Union is an international Christian charity working with churches in more than 130 countries.
Thank you for purchasing this resource. Any profits from this book support SU in England and Wales to bring the good news of Jesus Christ to children, young people and families and to enable them to meet God through the Bible and prayer.

Find out more about our work and how you can get involved at:
www.scriptureunion.org.uk (England and Wales)
www.suscotland.org.uk (Scotland)
www.suni.co.uk (Northern Ireland)
www.scriptureunion.org (USA)
www.su.org.au (Australia)

Acknowledgements

The Explore Together journey has been an exciting one but never has it been a solitary desktop endeavour. It was born out of practice, developed from questions asked and challenges faced. Throughout the journey there have been many people who have contributed to its development, sometimes without even knowing. It is to those people that we want to offer our thanks. To great thinkers like John H Westerhoff II, James Fowler, Rebecca Nye and Jerome Berryman who have opened our minds to new ways of thinking. To the many children who have taught us far more than we could ever have taught you, and to the amazing teams we have worked with over the years who have willingly and patiently supported and encouraged our desire to do things differently and push the boundaries.

Our practical thanks goes to Darren Hill, Terry Clutterham and Alan Charter for recognising the potential of Explore Together and for encouraging and enabling us to share it with you.

Lee expresses thanks to his church families down the years who fanned into flame his faith and love for God. 'I might not have known God if you had not reached, taught and nurtured me.'

Lianne wants to express special thanks to Phoebe and Jacob. 'You have taught me so much about so many things, being your mum has given me wings. Thank you for always believing in me.'

Finally, to our families and friends, thank you for your love and support.

'Now to him who is able to do immeasurably more than all we ask or imagine, according to his power that is at work within us, to him be glory in the church and in Christ Jesus throughout all generations, for ever and ever! Amen.' Ephesians 3:20,21

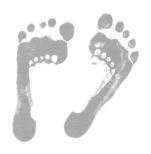

Contents

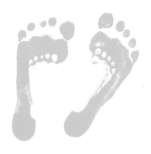

Foreword

'How can I use the Bible to reach out beyond the church?', 'How can I get our church members actually to relate to each other? To be a real community across the different age groups?', 'How can I get young people to join in?', 'How can I encourage Christians to grow stronger in their faith?', 'How will they ever gain an appetite for the Bible?', 'How can I find out what gifts people have?', 'How can I help people be more confident in talking about their faith?'

Two words: Explore Together.

'When two or three of you are together because of me, you can be sure that I'll be there,' said Jesus (Matthew 18:20, The Message). That's what makes Explore Together so compelling and so life-changing – the presence of God himself at work in and among people of any age, background, understanding and style, as they listen for him to speak with them through the Bible. No one truly experiences that and stays the same.

Last year my wife Sue and I used Explore Together at the Scripture Union holiday we run for families. In a field by a stream in a forest, everyone sleeps in log cabins, enjoying the fresh, clean, outdoor life.

There, parents and children play and try new things together, far away from the usual pressures and routines. And there they also explore the Bible and have the opportunity to respond to it, individually, in families and all together, many of them not used to doing so before they arrived.

For Explore Together times, everyone – 7-year-olds to 70s – came together as we set the scene for the Bible passage and picked up on the big questions for our Bible exploration. They set off individually, or with family or friends, to one or more of the ET zones. When they returned, they gathered first with their families to share what they had done and learnt, and then with the full group as we waited to hear what God had been saying.

Everyone hushed to listen. In response to the Bible, someone had created fabulous art; a young child had prayed; a teenager had chatted with a group about the issues in her life that the verses touched on; a 70-year-old had written a beautiful poem. You could have heard a pin drop. Every item was applauded; all contributions were valued; we saw how everything helped us. People carried on talking about the contributions throughout the day as God continued to work among us.

Whenever I have experienced Explore Together, the same things have struck me – whether with a bunch of families on a holiday, or at Spring Harvest with hundreds of children and leaders, or with team members together at a conference, or with a group of young people in a regular weekly session. Explore Together takes everyone seriously, whatever their age, as people who can explore the Bible in their own way and hear from God, who understand the importance and the potential of what they're doing and who know that, by telling others what they discover, everyone can be helped to grow stronger in their faith.

Somehow people recognise Explore Together as a big, very special, very spiritual moment.

So I fully endorse Explore Together as a simple but inspiring way to build up God's people – and those to whom they seek to reach out – through the Bible and prayer. I hope and pray that you will have the biggest, boldest adventures with it. Maybe you'll use Explore Together in contexts where at first you doubt it will ever work, but then you'll recall how God has always stepped in before and made the occasions so much more than you ever dreamed of. And you'll give it a try anyway. God is faithful, and he will be there among you.

Terry Clutterham
January 2015

Introduction

Have you ever had a real light-bulb moment? That exciting point in time where everything falls into place and makes perfect sense. Explore Together is the result of one such moment for us. Well, actually, it was more of a gradual turning on of a light bulb using a dimmer switch process; let me explain.

It all began in 2006. Lee and I were having one of our many 'putting the world to rights' conversations during a coffee break at a conference that we were attending together as fellow children's ministry practitioners and friends. We have known each other for many years, working together on children's camps and other events.

At that time Lee was employed by the Salvation Army as the children's officer for the central south of England, and I was working in a voluntary capacity as a children's worker in a local church. I was also a full-time mum and had taken the opportunity to engage in studying for a degree in children's and youth work. Both Lee and I have a background in education: I trained as a nursery nurse and worked in early years and Lee trained and worked as a primary school teacher and a leading teacher within the local authority.

Between us we had clocked a total of 40 years' experience of working with children in a professional and voluntary capacity.

Lee and I would often talk to each other about the difficulties and challenges we faced in our ministries, and we would also share our triumphs and successes. Between us we had most of the theoretical bases covered. We had a solid grasp of theory and practice around child development and learning. We understood the significance of the works of Piaget, Bruner, Skinner, Vygotsky and Gardner.

We had heard and even trained others on much of the theory around faith development and spiritual formation. We were well versed in the works of Fowler, Westerhoff and Nye. We were like sponges, buying every book and attending every seminar and conference that could possibly help us to be the best children's practitioners we could be. We were desperate to see the children and young people that we worked with grow in their faith, love the Bible and become committed followers of Jesus.

Although we were both seeing some great things happening in our ministries, we were very aware that we were only catching a tiny glimpse of the treasure God wanted to share with us. The possibilities and potential were driving us to want more for our young people!

It was Albert Einstein who defined insanity as doing the same thing over and over again and expecting different results. Lee and I had, over the years, introduced different elements into our programmes – great creative prayer opportunities, funky action songs with fun dance moves, interactive storytelling experiences, DVD clips, live bands, flags and ribbons – but the reality was we were still working within the same structure that we had worked with for years.

Lee talks about that time as being a time of huge frustration. He could see the increasing progress children were making in school by introducing small changes to his practice; he had seen for himself the power of personalisation, choice and children 'owning their learning'. On one hand he could see the potency of such elements in his teaching, but felt unable to apply them in a children's ministry setting. Children's work in church was still very didactic, generic and managed by the leaders.

What we both offered in our ministry was still very much a one-size-fits-all approach. The epiphany moment came to us when we seriously asked ourselves the questions: What would our children's ministry look like if we put all of the theories that we had spent years studying into practice? What would happen if we applied in church the excellent practice we had employed in our work with children outside of a children's ministry context?

I said earlier that our light-bulb moment was more like the turning up of a dimmer switch. This was the point that we turned that switch.

We began to work through our challenges and apply the theories to them. These included:

- managing groups with wide age ranges
- catering for groups of varying sizes
- managing difficult and challenging behaviour
- catering for a range of learning preferences and learning needs
- supporting parents within the church to recognise their responsibility for nurturing faith in their children.

What we discovered wasn't ground-breaking, in fact, it was comforting in its simplicity.

It didn't require us to do much more than create a safe environment where God's voice could be heard, and to step back and trust him to speak.

As Explore Together began to emerge we quickly saw the impact that it had on our groups. It encouraged:

- community building
- Bible engagement
- faith formation
- growth in discipleship
- inclusivity.

We recognised that God had given us a gift and we wanted to share it.

In 2009 we introduced Explore Together to the 8 to 11s children's programme at Spring Harvest. By this time, Lee had returned to teaching and I had taken up a full-time position with Scripture Union as a church and community development worker. The children's programme at Spring Harvest was part of my role.

Lee and I knew that Explore Together worked well within a small group setting, it had been tried and tested and we trusted the theories enough to introduce it to this programme. So, with 450 8- to 11-year-olds and a team of 60 volunteers, we set off.

On the first night, we presented the Bible story and sent the children off to explore the questions in the different zones that we had prepared. We knew that it could work brilliantly, but we were slightly nervous that it could also end in chaos so, with a contingency plan up our sleeves, the two of us went back stage to pray. Let's just say, we didn't need to use our contingency plan. The power of the Holy Spirit moved in that chilly venue every night that week as the children and the team heard from God and learned from each other. The results were powerful and inspiring, with many children and team members feeding back at the end of the week that Explore Together had been their highlight. Team members went away itching to introduce it into their own children's programmes. The light bulb was getting brighter, but the brightest moment was yet to come.

All-age worship was beginning to feature quite prominently in my local church ministry and also in my role with Scripture Union. I would quite often be asked to lead all-age services at my church, and in my Scripture Union capacity I was often asked to run training sessions on 'How to lead all-age services'. In fact, the all-age sessions at conferences almost always attracted the most delegates.

I knew that the volunteers we had worked with at Spring Harvest had really engaged with Explore Together alongside the children, many experiencing profound encounters with God both directly and through the things that the children had shared. With this in mind, I began to use Explore Together in all-age settings. I quickly realised that the theories that we put into practice within our children's programmes were theories that applied to every age and stage of our faith formation. Explore Together really did release intergenerational communities to discover the Bible together at the same time, in the same place and it was truly beautiful.

The light-bulb moment? Well, that came when we embraced Jesus' words, '… unless you change and become like little children, you will never enter the kingdom of heaven' (Matthew 18:3). Explore Together works because it helps us to rediscover what children haven't lost yet: elements that enable them to connect with God in ways that some of us have grown out of.

Elements like awe, wonder, creative exploration and interdependency.

In her book *The Seed and the Soil*, Pauline Hoggarth stresses the importance of the word 'creative', stating that 'the church needs to take seriously the fact that people learn in different ways, and adapt its approaches accordingly'.[1] She suggests that, 'there needs to be a continuum between our Bible engagement approaches with younger generation and with adults ... engaging with God's word as adults often becomes too focused on analytical, propositional thinking and ignores the intuitive and imaginative aspects of the person.'[2]

By placing children at the centre of our thinking, studying how they learn, develop and grow in their faith, Lee and I were able to reconnect to the very heart of who we are. We are children of God, dependent on a continued and close relationship with our heavenly Father, created in his image, connected to each other as brothers and sisters, dependent on each other for growth. We are all one in Jesus Christ (Galatians 3:28).

We would both now find it hard to plan any event for children, young people or adults, churched or unchurched, that did not include an opportunity to explore together. Lee has continued to develop Explore Together within the context of the school where he is deputy head teacher, and I have used it in a multitude of settings, including sessions for teenagers and adult house groups.

This book is a chronicle of our journey so far. The first three chapters address the question, 'Why do we need to explore together?', investigating the practical, theoretical and biblical

---

1 Pauline Hoggarth, *The Seed and the Soil*, Global Christian Library, 2011 p123
2 ibid, p124

contexts. The final three chapters focus on the question, 'What does exploring together involve?'

Our journey with Explore Together has revealed so much to us about the way in which God communicates with us, through his Word and through his community. We invite you to join us as we continue on that journey, and discover for yourselves how you can explore together in your own communities. We hope and pray that Explore Together will become a useful and valuable tool in your ministry toolkit.

> *Commit to the Lord whatever you do, and he will establish your plans.*
>
> *Proverbs 16:3*

Chapter 1

Journeying together

Choice is perceived as a fundamental right in today's society. We shop around for the best deals; we know what we like and, with the internet at our fingertips, we know exactly where we can get it.

Many of us look for churches in the same way. We have a list of boxes that we're looking to tick. If we have young children it goes without saying that we are going to look for a church that has a vibrant and fun programme of activities to offer them. If we don't, that might be the last thing on our list. We have all either used or heard phrases like: 'We tried that church but there were no other 20s to 30s' or 'We trawled their website and couldn't find an inclusions policy'.

We shop around for something that best fits our requirements and sometimes, if we can't find the right thing, we'll start our own church. And why not? After all, we are just searching for an environment where we can deepen our relationship with God and experience a real sense of belonging and acceptance.

Over the years the church has tried to meet all these different needs, reaching out to those for whom church is a familiar place and those who have never been before.

Messy Church, for example, was developed in response to the need to engage with families who had no serious connection to a church.[1] The Kidz Klub[2] model encourages churches to connect with the children in their communities by providing a bus service to bring them to weekly events. In addition, every child who attends Kidz Klub receives a home visit each week prior to the event.

Scripture Union offers X:site, designed to equip local churches to work together to provide a bi-monthly event that supports and encourages young junior-school-aged Christians to bring their friends to hear about Jesus in exciting and culturally relevant ways.[3] There are also a plethora of men's groups, women's groups, youth churches all with the same aim: to make the good news of Jesus known within the sections of society that are currently unreached.

As the demand for new ideas and resources increased so did the number of conferences that cater for the many and varied areas of ministry. Local churches began to employ specialists to ensure that they could offer the very best provision to all members of the community. In response to this, local Bible colleges developed courses that award professional qualifications in outreach, family ministries, children's and youth work, Third Age ministries and more.

The church now has a workforce of highly skilled professionals educated to certificate, diploma, degree and PhD level running and resourcing our local church ministries. We are a church doing all that we can to provide every possible opportunity for all people from every age and stage of life to 'move beyond the

1 Paul Moore, *Making Disciples in Messy Church*, The Bible Reading Fellowship, 2013
2 www.kidzklubwindsor.co.uk
3 www.xsiteuk.org

elementary teachings about Christ and be taken forward to maturity'.[4]

There are many who would applaud this evolution of the church, but attendance figures[5] and various research findings[6] would suggest that this approach is not achieving the desired outcomes, especially for our younger generations. It would appear that, in our attempts to meet the needs of all, we have removed an essential faith-growing ingredient; one that has the potential to breathe life and vitality into the dry bones of a head-based faith. That ingredient is 'togetherness'.

Despite a pursuit of separateness, the church in general is not ignorant of the need for togetherness. There has been a real drive to create regular opportunities to unite the dispersed community in worship and teaching. Simple!

Well, actually, it isn't that simple at all. We have become so conditioned in our belief that separate is best that when faced with the task of planning for such an occasion we panic. The research tells us that these times of togetherness are essential. The conference experts tell us that we need to make sure we are creating times of togetherness. But the reality can be the cold-sweat-inducing stuff of nightmares.

'All-age service' becomes a regular entry in our church diary so that we can tick the 'togetherness' box, but whose responsibility is it? We may have a number of professional employees; a

---

4 Hebrews 6:1

5 A 2005 survey found 39% of Anglican churches had no one attending under the age of 11, 49% had no 11 to 14s in attendance and 59% had no 15- to 19-year-olds in their congregations

6 Just 5% of children in the UK attend church regularly, and schools teach little more than the basics about Christianity (based on Peter Brierley (editor), *UK Church Statistics 2005–2015*, Brierley Consulting, 2010, and national and local government census statistics 2011)

children's worker who knows how children tick; a youth worker who understands how teenagers are wired; a family worker who understands the needs of parents in varying models of family units. That is, of course, if our church is fortunate enough to be in a position to employ these people. There are approximately 90 churches in the town where I live and only eight of those employ a youth or children's worker. The reality for most is that of a paid minister and a group of willing volunteers – all hoping that they are not the one who draws the short straw on the 'all-age' rota.

At best, all-age services can be pleasant, light-hearted breaks in the calendar where the adults get to participate in or observe a children's service with Bible quizzes, games, DVDs and funky action songs. At worst they are cringeworthy and uncomfortable affairs which induce an exodus effect on people, who seize the opportunity to arrange visits to family when they see 'all-age' appear on the church notice sheet.

However, it isn't all doom and gloom. Many churches have a really positive approach to togetherness and strive to embrace every opportunity to bring the community together. Celebrations and social events build relationships across the generations, which in turn makes those times of coming together for worship and teaching a much more natural experience. Edward's church, for instance:

Story

Edward was born into a church community that really embraces togetherness. The congregation in his church numbers 50 to 80 and includes a variety of ages from birth to 90. Throughout his 17 years[7] the children and young people in

---

7 The age of Edward when this book went to press

his church community have always been present throughout the Sunday morning and evening services. The services last for an hour and include singing, testimony, prayer, storytelling, choir, a brass band and a sermon.

At 7 years old Edward became a member of the children's choir, which makes a weekly valued contribution to the church worship and meets together for a midweek rehearsal. Until he was old enough to listen, during the 20-minute sermons Edward, along with his younger sister and all of the other children, would draw, read and eat snacks. He has always felt that he is part of what is going on. After the morning service there is time for a drink and a biscuit with everyone together, and then the children's and youth groups meet for an hour.

In addition to the Sunday services, the church meets together regularly for picnics, walks, barn dances and special occasions. Edward has friends of all ages, they all know his name and Edward knows theirs. It is because of the 'together' nature of his church that Edward and the other children feel comfortable and welcome (albeit a bit fidgety at times) when they are in the church services and, on the occasions when services that celebrate the children in their church are held (three times a year), the adults feel comfortable and welcome too, always willing to participate in quizzes, dramas and games.

Edward is currently studying for A levels at college. He is a very active and valued member of his church community and has a very strong faith of his own. 'All-age' never appears on his church calendar because his church is 'all-age'.

The introduction of Messy Church in 2004 has gone some way towards cultivating a new mindset of togetherness that endorses the view that we are indeed, in the words of Alistair Darling, 'better together'.[8] Messy Church is reaching families with no previous experience of church services and welcoming them through the doors by declaring that it is a way of being church for families that is fun. Its values are about being Christ-centred, for all ages, based on creativity, hospitality and celebration. The challenge, however, that many Messy Church communities are facing is that they limit themselves to only attracting families with young children. Other groups who may not have any natural association with young children would probably not be drawn to a Messy service.

So why is it just so difficult to get 'all-age' right? Why is it that a large percentage of our congregations would rather be anywhere else than attending an all-age service? Why does it just have to be a box-ticking exercise and not the highlight of the calendar month?

The answer to all of these questions is the same. Since the church adopted Robert Raikes' Sunday school model to educate children in the Christian faith in 1870,[9] we have fallen into a very deep trap of believing that the best way for everyone to learn about the faith is in age-specific groups. It's best for parents so that they can enjoy an interruption-free time of worship and teaching. Its best for babies and toddlers because they get to move about and play freely. It's best for children because they get to learn according to their educational age level and be with their friends. It's best for teenagers because

8 Strapline of the Scottish referendum 2014
9 This was not the original intended purpose of the Sunday School Movement. Its original purpose in 1780 was to teach the illiterate lower classes to read and write on the only day off they had in their working week. Sunday schools taught predominantly children but often adults too using the Bible as their main educational source. In 1870 the Education Act was introduced and this service was no longer necessary. The church kept the model to teach catechesis to their children and from there it evolved

teenagers... well teenagers are just teenagers and no one apart from the experts really understands their needs.

In response to this historical conditioning and, more recently, the development in the 1970s of the homogeneous unit principle,[10] we resource and endorse separate groups for faith formation. It may be perceived to be the easiest way, but it certainly isn't the best.

Story

Let me introduce you to Poppy. Poppy is the only child of Greg and Anna. Greg worked late shifts at a local manufacturing plant. Anna worked as an administrative assistant at a local college. Their joint income wasn't great but they got by. Poppy was entitled to a discounted place at the college day nursery, attended from 8.30am to 4.30pm every day from age 3 months to when she started school. Greg, Anna and Poppy lived a considerable distance from their extended family, so Poppy didn't get to see her grandparents as much as Greg and Anna would have liked.

The family attended the local church together, although Greg didn't always get there because of his shift work. The service began with a welcome, a hymn, prayer, the church notices, then the offering was taken up, during which the children and young people left the congregation to attend their groups. Once a month the children and young people started off in their groups but joined the rest of the congregation at the end of the service for communion.

---

10 Originally described by Donald A McGraven in relation to church growth, endorsing the necessity for churches to engage with specific cultures, eg youth, ethnic, goth, as a means of authentic mission

The church wasn't huge in number but there was a good-sized group of children of various ages in attendance. Poppy attended the crèche every Sunday morning from being a babe in arms. The other babies and toddlers in the crèche were not there as regularly as she was. Each Sunday she was cared for by different ladies on the rota; they were all very lovely and she was content to play with the toys while the Julia Plaut CD played in the background.

When Poppy was 3 she started going to a different group, which was for pre-schoolers, and the helpers were different ladies from the ones in crèche. There were four other children there but she didn't see them every week; Poppy really liked playing with Muriel, she was smiley and fun. Gluing and painting were also fun, and Poppy loved story time. Every week at the end of Sunday school she put a colourful activity sheet into her mummy's bag; she's not sure what happened to it after that.

When Poppy started school everything changed. She stopped going to her nursery every day. Her school was bigger and noisier. There were no babies there. Poppy really liked the babies at nursery; she really liked Julie too. Julie was Poppy's key worker, who had looked after her every day. Poppy loved her, but she wasn't going to see her any more.

Poppy took a while to settle in to school and she didn't really want to go into the new 4 to 7s group at church either. Every Sunday she would cry when someone tried to take her to the group; they had to let her mummy go with her until she settled down. Muriel wasn't in this group, although Poppy did sometimes see her in big church and they waved to each other. Poppy liked Muriel best. There were seven other children in the group when Poppy joined, and after a while she really started to like it; she made friends with Billy and Ella. She enjoyed learning actions to some new fun songs and she really loved that they had lots of space to do running around games. Ella didn't like the running around games. Billy moved up to the 8 to 11s group before Poppy and Ella did, and they missed him. Poppy missed him the most because he was more fun than Ella, who didn't really like joining in much.

By the time Poppy went up into the next group both Billy and Ella had stopped coming to church; she never saw either of them again. Poppy was looking forward to the older group, though, because the little ones in her group really got on her nerves now. The 8 to 11s group had nine children in it when everyone was there, five boys and three other girls. The boys were really stupid. They didn't listen and they got told off a lot. Poppy enjoyed the quizzes because she knew a lot of the answers as she knew loads of Bible stories. The grown-ups were nice, too, although she never really knew who was going to be there and it was sometimes difficult to remember their names.

When Poppy was 10 her world fell apart. Her mum and dad got a divorce. Poppy knew that lots of her school friends' parents were divorced but she never thought it would happen to hers. Poppy just didn't know what to do. She kept going to church with her mum but she felt really uncomfortable when her mum cried in front of everyone and people put their arms around her. Going out to Sunday school was always a relief because nobody mentioned it in there. Poppy joined in with everything but she wasn't sure that God was an actual thing any more. However much she prayed for her dad to come home, he never did. If God was real surely he would listen and make everything OK? Home was horrible, church was confusing; the only place that Poppy felt safe and comfortable was at school. School made sense. She saw the same people every day and they knew her really well. Her favourite teacher would ask her if she was OK, and on the rare occasions when Poppy got upset her teacher would take her to a nice quiet room and they would have good chats about everything. Her teacher never mentioned God, she was just kind. Her friends never mentioned God either and they were so much fun to be with. She liked being at school the best.

Then another change! A horrible big change: secondary school. Once again Poppy had to leave a place of security that she loved to step into an unknown. Her two best friends were in a different from her, and some of her other friends had gone to different schools. Saying goodbye to her favourite teacher made her heart hurt so bad. She cried in her room for ages. She also had to start catching the bus on her own.

Home was still tough, her mum was doing OK but Poppy still heard her crying at night sometimes. Her dad had a girlfriend. Poppy hated her. Church was OK, she and two of the boys went up into the youth group – another bunch of adults on a rota to get to know. At least she only had to go every other week now because she went to her dad's on the other weekends and he didn't go to church at all any more. The girlfriend had her own little girl who was actually quite cute, so Poppy spent all of her time playing with her when she stayed there.

Youth group was OK; there was always something to eat, which was a bonus. The youth worker, Chelle, was really nice but she left after a year because she got a job with a different church. The church didn't get another youth worker to replace her. There were some really good bits about the youth group and they did have a laugh, but most of the time Poppy was really irritated when she went there. They never talked about the stuff that bothered Poppy and she didn't want to ask, like, Will my dad go to hell? What about evolution? My best friend's mum is a lesbian, does God hate her?

Poppy continued to go to church with her mum, but when it came to GCSEs and A levels she played the, 'I need to revise' card until she barely went to church at all.

Poppy was always very clever and she worked very hard at school. Working helped her not to focus too much on the things she hated about her life, and as a consequence she did really well in all of her exams, earning herself a place at university where she studied biochemistry.

Poppy left church with very little fanfare; she was the only one in the youth group leaving to go to university that year. The other two boys who had joined the group with her had left the church. They did both go to university, though, because the vicar mentioned them when he asked the people in church to pray for Poppy.

That was actually the last time Poppy went to church, apart from at Christmas when she stayed with her mum, and by then her mum had moved away to be closer to her parents and was going to a different church.

When we unpick Poppy's story we can see that 15 minutes of 'togetherness' at the beginning of the church service was not enough for her to develop a sense of community, identity or belonging. There were essential elements missing from Poppy's life that had they been present could have made a world of difference to her faith.

The places that Poppy felt most secure in her childhood were nursery and primary school. There were no male role models in either of those places and her own father was absent much of the time, even before he left the family home, due to working hours. Poppy didn't have the opportunity to develop relationships with members of the older generations as her own grandparents lived away from her and there weren't any older people in her school or nursery. Poppy was always surrounded by other children of her own age, but she never spent a lot of time with other age groups apart from her dad's girlfriend's little girl.

The faith community that Poppy grew up in had the potential to meet and fulfil every need that Poppy had to belong and grow in her faith but, in their pursuit of what they believed to be the best way, Poppy lost her way.

Unfortunately, this story is true, and there are many other similar stories. The church is haemorrhaging children and young people at an alarming rate,[11] and unless we start to foster an attitude of togetherness that models biblical community we cannot hope to reverse this devastating trend.

A biblical community

So, what does a biblical community look like? What are the characteristics that distinguish it from any other community? A biblical community is:

Focused on God

This may seem like the most obvious characteristic, but it's worth reminding ourselves what this actually looks like. God

---

11 1,000 under 15s are leaving the church each week (Peter Brierley, *The Tide is Running Out: What the English Church Attendance Survey Reveals*, Christian Research, 2000, p98)

In 1900 55% of children attended church regularly; by 2000 this figure had dropped to 4% (*UK Christian Handbook of Religious Trends*, Christian Research, 2001, section 2, p15)

and the Bible are the foundation of a biblical community. He is worthy of our praise and adoration, he is Father, Son and Spirit, the focus of our whole being. He is love (1 John 4:8). When that focus shifts from our mighty and powerful God to our own desires and needs the community suffers; when it remains we become more like the community he created us to be.

Hearing that Jesus had silenced the Sadducees, the Pharisees got together. One of them, an expert in the law, tested him with this question: 'Teacher, which is the greatest commandment in the Law?'

Jesus replied: '"Love the Lord your God with all your heart and with all your soul and with all your mind." This is the first and greatest commandment. And the second is like it: "Love your neighbour as yourself." All the Law and the Prophets hang on these two commandments.'

Matthew 22:34–40

It is only when we truly know God that we can make him truly known. It is only when we fully understand the extent of the love that God has for us and the world that he created that we can fully love others. Without love, we are nothing (1 Corinthians 13).

A glimpse of heaven
A biblical community brings heaven to earth, pointing the world to God and modelling love, forgiveness, acceptance, grace and favour. It brings hope to the hopeless, comfort and healing to the sick and broken, it demands justice for the oppressed.

Once, on being asked by the Pharisees when the kingdom of God would come, Jesus replied, 'The coming of the kingdom of God is not something that can be observed, nor will people say, "Here it is," or "There it is," because the kingdom of God is in your midst.'

Luke 17:20,21

A biblical community paints a beautiful picture of what God wants to restore us to (Revelation 21:1–5).

Family

Hear, O Israel: The Lord our God, the Lord is one. Love the Lord your God with all your heart and with all your soul and with all your strength. These commandments that I give you today are to be on your hearts. Impress them on your children. Talk about them when you sit at home and when you walk along the road, when you lie down and when you get up. Tie them as symbols on your hands and bind them on your foreheads. Write them on the doorframes of your houses and on your gates.

Deuteronomy 6:4–9

This verse is often quoted in reference to Christian parenting, and some would use it to suggest that the responsibility for the faith formation of children rests firmly with their biological parents. In many cases, the church today has moved towards an understanding that faith formation is also the responsibility of children's and youth workers, in partnership with the parents. No! Even this doesn't reflect what Moses meant. When delivering this speech Moses was addressing the whole of the nation, and placing the duty of passing on the faith to the children firmly at their collective feet. God's plan, seen in Deuteronomy 6, is that the faith community should support the family and together they nurture the children. In doing so, the children will see many adults living in loving obedience to God. They can ask questions of the people they admire and hear stories of God at work. A biblical community strengthens parents and enables children to grow in their commitment to God.

> *At that time the disciples came to Jesus and asked, 'Who, then, is the greatest in the kingdom of heaven?' He called a little child to him, and placed the child among them. And he said: 'Truly I tell you, unless you change and become like little children, you will never enter the kingdom of heaven. Therefore, whoever takes the lowly position of this child is the greatest in the kingdom of heaven. And whoever welcomes one such child in my name welcomes me.'*
>
> *Matthew 18:1–5*

These five verses teach us so much about the family aspect of a biblical community. The most glaringly obvious part of this lesson is that Jesus called out to the child. It doesn't say that Jesus sent one of his disciples to fetch a child from the children's area where another of the disciples who was particularly gifted with children was teaching them. The child was there in the crowd, with everyone else. Therefore, the child was hearing the questions of the adults and was part of Jesus' answer. Finally and most importantly, Jesus teaches us that children play a vital role in our understanding of faith. If they are removed from our midst, how will we ever know how to become like them? A biblical community challenges us to commit ourselves to life together as a people of God so that we may all 'grow up in Christ'.

Authentic community

Living in a biblical community provides every member at every age and stage in their journey with:

- a way to see Christ in others (John 13:34; 15:2)
- a source of accountability and guidance where we can learn from each other (Colossians 3:9)
- lessons in handling difficult relationships, family, money, spiritual growth and struggles, success and failure (Galatians 6:1,2)
- a place where we can experiment with and learn the life of prayer; being a spectator is not enough, we must learn to be active participants (Ephesians 6:18)
- a place to serve one another and in doing so grow stronger in Christ (John 13:1–20; Galatians 5:13)
- the strength to be witnesses in the world (Matthew 5:13–16)
- the ability to be ambassadors of God's love in our wider communities (Micah 6:8)
- a focus on relationships, through which God seeks to pour out his love on us all (Genesis 2:18; Ecclesiastes 4:9–12).

The early church met together frequently; they were a deeply constant presence in each other's lives.

They devoted themselves to the apostles' teaching and to fellowship, to the breaking of bread and to prayer. Everyone was filled with awe at the many wonders and signs performed by the apostles. All the believers were together and had everything in common. They sold property and possessions to give to anyone who had need. Every day they continued to meet together in the temple courts. They broke bread in their homes and ate together with glad and sincere hearts, praising God and enjoying the favour of all the people.

Acts 2:42–47

Occasional or infrequent gatherings just don't have the same impact on growth and maturity. A gathering of people who don't really know each other are not authentically a biblical community.

Poppy's experience of church was not one that immersed her into a biblical community. There were so many elements that were missing for her. The following story draws together elements of some amazing practical examples of biblical community and togetherness that I have personally encountered in various Christian communities that I have had the privilege of visiting and being part of in the UK. Together they present a picture of what a healthy church family could look like.

Worship in this church is an exciting, colourful celebration of who God is and what he is currently doing. It recognises but does not dwell on what he has done in the past. Musicians, dancers, artists and poets are embraced and every element of diversity is celebrated in the presence of God and the community. Members of the community of all ages are invited regularly to finish the sentence, 'This time tomorrow I will be...'. By doing this everyone gets to know each other and has some understanding of what their brothers and sisters in Christ do when they're not at a church service. Sometimes what they share is exciting, sometimes mundane and sometimes difficult, but each person is prayed for and known by the others.

Key Christian festivals and occasions are taken seriously, as much emphasis and importance is placed on the big story of faith.

In this community times of transition are marked with a VIP

banquet every September. Every child and young person transitioning from one place to another receives a VIP invitation, and the whole community marks that occasion with words of encouragement, stories of their own experiences, delicious food and partying.

Faith formation begins in the home, with families being supported and encouraged to foster and nurture whole-life discipleship. Christian parenting is a partnership between parents and other members of the Christian community. This church has adopted the 5:1 principle,[12] where every child and young person has five people of different generations actively involved in their lives beyond the church service. For example, Thomas, aged 15, and his parents invited the following people, who were already known and trusted by the family, to intentionally support him in his faith formation:

John, aged 40 – A member of the youth team who is a carpenter by trade and shares Thomas' sense of humour and love of all things Marvel and DC. John has trained as a mentor on the church's mentoring programme and meets with Thomas monthly, with the permission of his parents, often over a curry, when they talk about school, home, faith and the future. In between those times they are just mates and occasional cinema buddies (also with his parents' permission).

Janet, aged 61 – Janet is a larger than life huggy lady with a big heart and a lot of love to give. Thomas chose Janet because she has always spoken to him at church. She was delighted that Thomas wanted her to be part of his journey; she has now added sweets, treats and occasional phone calls to her weekly distribution of hugs and happiness. Thomas knows that Janet prays for him.

---

12 Kara Powell & Chap Clark, *Sticky Faith*, Zondervan, 2011, p103

Arthur, aged 72 – Arthur is a retired financial adviser who again was chosen by Thomas because of the genuine interest he has shown in Thomas' life. Thomas wanted to grow vegetables, and both of his parents were horticulturally challenged. Arthur helped Thomas to dig and grow a vegetable patch and they bought seeds together. Arthur's grandchildren live abroad and Thomas' only remaining grandfather lives a long way away. Thomas gets to see what it means to be a 70+ man of God and Arthur gets to be a granddad.

Sam, aged 23 – Sam is the coolest musician Thomas knows. He plays the guitar and drums in the worship band. Thomas wanted to learn to play guitar and Sam lives on his own. Sam comes round for a cooked meal once a week and gives Thomas a guitar lesson while the dinner is cooking. Sam gets fed and Thomas gets to play in the worship band and learn what it's like to become a young man of God.

Melissa, aged 28 (and Paul) – Melissa and Paul are a young married couple. Melissa has known Thomas for a very long time and they have a great friendship; Paul came along and they got married. Thomas loves Paul and Melissa and they love him. They were delighted to be part of his journey.

Even if Thomas were to decide to leave the church, these people would still be very much part of his life, keeping him connected to the community, practically, and prayerfully journeying with him.

In this church group teaching is still part of the programme, but equally valued are the regular times where the whole community come together to share a meal and explore the Word of God.

In this church nothing is done apart that could be done together.

What difference would being part of a Christian community like this have made to the lives of Poppy, Anna and Greg? Of course this is a hypothetical question, but it serves to help us to think a little about what 'together' really means.

Whether we like it or not, whether we think it's wrong or right, the reality for many churches in the UK is that we segregate more than we gather together. What this story highlights is that togetherness needs to be more than a box-ticking exercise that slots an all-age service into our calendar once a month. Togetherness is about intentionally cultivating a mindset within our Christian communities that takes seriously its collective responsibility for faith formation and helps each member of that community recognise the part that they have to play in that process. It's a mindset that needs to embrace the diversity of God's created people, drawing together the richness of that diversity to create an experience of mutual benefit: an environment where everyone feels accepted and where everyone has the best opportunity to reach maturity.

It is our hope that, through the remaining chapters of this book, we will be able to dispel the fear that grips us when we start to try and think of ways in which we can come together as a whole church around God's Word. We hope that we will be able to help you to experience the joy and inspiration that comes when we make time to hear from God as a whole community and learn from each other as we journey together.

Reflect

If you would find it helpful, use the following questions and writing spaces to reflect on the ideas in this chapter.

1 Do you agree that 'togetherness' is a key faith-growing ingredient? Why, or why not?

2 In what ways have you seen your church/community pursue 'separateness'? What are the advantages and disadvantages of a 'separate' approach?

3 How can separateness and togetherness exist harmoniously in a church community?

4 How do you feel about all-age services? What has led you to feel this way?

5 What would need to be different to make an all-age service the highlight of your week/month?

6 What can you learn from Poppy's story? How might this influence your practice?

7 Which of the characteristics of a biblical community do you see exhibited in your church/community? Are there any other characteristics you might like to add?

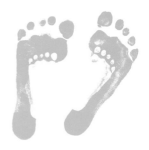

Chapter 2

The challenges of being together

2

Coming together as a whole church around God's Word is a significant challenge. Being together presents demands on all of us, whether in church or out of it.

A family Christmas meal has the potential to be a beautifully precious opportunity for family members. You can imagine the scene: the older members of the family delighting in being surrounded by those in whom they have invested over the years, and the children excitedly sharing their gifts with each other. The Christmas meal allows time for exciting celebration, much relished catching-up, enjoying each other's company, reminiscing over family stories and partaking in the most delicious food.

Equally the Christmas meal has the potential to achieve the opposite and create the feeling of sheer dread: family members gathering together who have completely different tastes in food; young and old family members who cannot bear spending time together; children fighting over their new gifts, totally unwilling to share; older generations irritated by the demanding children; and individuals who are really just counting down the hours until they can get on with their ordinary, very separate lives.

The extremes outlined in the descriptions of the Christmas meals represent both the value and the challenges of togetherness. Being together in family life has strong semblance to sharing life in a faith community. Chapter 1 clearly outlines the necessity of being together, counteracting the prevailing church culture of age-group segregation. It also lays down some defining features of biblical community. However, it is important for us to be clear that being together and growing faith together are not things we can achieve passively; togetherness demands more than just showing up, it requires a practical response to a number of significant challenges.

Challenge 1: We experience and express spirituality differently

Story

Ross came to Christian faith as an adult. His two children had found faith for themselves while attending the children's programmes at his local church. Soon after, Ross' wife made her own commitment to follow Jesus. She loved helping out with the children's programmes. Ross then got involved in helping out at church, playing football with the church team and supporting with maintenance jobs and technology. Eventually Ross, having spent numerous late nights battling with some of his own questions, chose to follow Jesus for himself.

After a few months, Ross found himself struggling to grow in his faith despite attending every church service and joining nearly every Bible study group. He could not connect with words that were being spoken and, although he understood the themes and messages communicated, he didn't feel they had any impact on his life. He expressed feeling a lack of fulfilment and feeling a desire to be close to God that had not been realised. This went on for some time, until he found himself leading a ministry to older people and families in the wider community, who needed practical support: window cleaning, bits of decorating, gardening, feeding those who had no food on a catering team. He also set up a football team and found his niche helping those outside of the church to understand the relevance of Jesus to them.

Ross explained that he felt that his faith was most alive when he was actively living it out, and seeing life lived out by those around him. He enjoyed 'being the difference' in the world that he had anticipated Jesus would make.

Ross is not unusual. He struggled to experience and express his faith in the ways that his church had established for him. David Csinos argues that, 'people require the freedom to connect with God in their own ways, and that ministries with children (and people of all ages) need to move beyond one size fits all approaches.' [11]

Csinos proposes a new way of thinking about how people experience and express their spirituality. He suggests four spiritual styles that are evident in those who are engaged in finding and making meaning in their lives. He maintains that these are 'a construction to aid understanding different ways that people know and experience God.' These styles provide 'distinct yet fluid and porous boundaries in which people live out their innate spirituality.'

1 David Csinos, *Children's Ministry that Fits*, Wipf & Stock, 2011, p50

Word-centred spirituality

This spiritual style is focused upon experiencing and expressing faith through words. An individual with this preference might excel in faith development when they are focused on increasing knowledge, reflecting on spiritual texts or sharing in words that are spoken or written.

Emotion-centred spirituality

Someone who has this spiritual style as a preference will strongly believe that engaging with God is most powerful when you are experiencing strong feelings and emotions. Csinos explains that music, drama and dance are particularly effective tools for those who demonstrate this style.

Symbol-centred spirituality

Those who love the mystery of faith embody this spiritual style. They seek to connect with God in symbol and ritual. An interest in art and the visual, an appreciation for the aesthetic and a love of using imagination might be evidence of this.

Action-centred spirituality

This preferred style has a focus upon how faith and spirituality are lived out in practice. Individuals who experience and express faith this way are concerned with how faith and spirituality get their 'sleeves rolled up' and bring positive change in the world.

Csinos advocates that, although we might find that we have strong personal preferences for a particular spiritual style, these styles overlap and influence each other. He suggests that throughout our lives and at different times our styles are changing; on our journey of faith these styles are fluid rather than fixed.

How could a model of worship and discipleship cater for this range of spiritual styles? Ross' church catered in ways that were strongly word-centred. Teaching in Bible studies and church services focused on what could be expressed verbally and in written form, and it could be argued that an action-centred spirituality would have enabled him to find fulfilment sooner. Ross found practical acts of service enabled him to know God better and live that out in the world. In serving older people he could identify with the love of God for people. In serving on the catering team he identified with Jesus' teaching on how, when we provide food for those who are hungry, we are actually feeding Jesus himself (Matthew 25:40). Finally, in helping with decorating, gardening and repairs he could physically see himself involved in acts of transformation.

How in church are we encouraged to discover our spiritual styles? I wonder how many people (like Ross) find themselves spiritually unfulfilled, and then leave the church before they have an opportunity to discover and develop their arguably God-given spiritual style.

Challenge 2: We learn differently

Story

Jonny became a Christian at the age of 15 at a church children's camp that he had been invited to help with. His parents were pastors in the church, but his view had always been 'Jesus and germs – can't see either, why should I be bothered about them?' Jonny felt that if he could not see it, he was not able to believe it.

Jonny had heard the Christian message over and over again in stories and teaching, but it had never made sense to him because it had not been something he could see for himself. At that camp he got to know a new Christian friend who lived and breathed Christian faith. Jonny had never listened to teaching and found it hard to concentrate. The camp had been monumental for him because he could see what being a Christian was about, and he wanted to be a part of it.

Although the Holy Spirit is primarily responsible for Jonny coming to faith, Jonny certainly feels that if the Christian message had been communicated in more than just words he would have come to faith sooner.

Much research has been done in recent years to expound the idea that, as individuals, we learn differently. A plethora of theoretical models have arisen, coming under the title of 'learning styles'. What these models have in common is the understanding that as individuals we absorb, process, comprehend and retain information in different ways.

Fleming's VARK model[2]

Neil Fleming explains that an individual's learning style is made up of more than 18 different elements. These include temperature, light, food intake, biorhythms, working with others and working alone. His popular research focuses upon one specific preference in learning – an individual's preferred way of receiving information and sharing information. He sees that there are four key modes of learning:

Visual

This learner prefers observing the gestures of a presenter. They enjoy language that is picturesque. They typically learn from diagrams, slides, pictures, charts, graphs and symbols.

2 Neil Fleming, *Teaching & Learning Styles: VARK Strategies*, 2001

Aural (auditory)

This learner prefers to listen to the examples, stories and ideas of a presenter. They engage with music and discussion and recording. They benefit from explaining new ideas and thoughts with others.

Reader/writer

This learner benefits from a presenter who provides notes and uses words well. They prefer learning using lists and note taking, often with headings. They will seek out dictionaries, glossaries, definitions and manuals.

Kinaesthetic

This learner prefers a multi-sensory approach. They benefit from hands-on experiences, trips, presenters who share real-life examples and learning through trial and error.

Fleming's VARK model also appreciates that many of us are multi-modal – we learn using a combination of the visual, auditory, reading/writing and kinaesthetic.

Although Fleming's work does not go unchallenged, the principle that underpins his work, that as individuals we learn in different ways and have personal modal preferences, is borne out visibly in everyday life. For example, why do some of us learn things more easily than others? Why can one verbal explanation prove satisfactory to one individual, but confound another? Why do some of us seemingly make better sense of a visual diagram, but others need to be actively involved in solving problems to truly understand?

Gardner's multiple intelligences

Howard Gardner presents an alternative approach to the personal and individual ways in which we learn.

Fleming considers how we process and make sense of the things we are learning about. Gardner's approach focuses upon how we demonstrate what we have learned. Gardner suggests that we each have a psychological make-up that determines how we demonstrate and apply what we know too.

Gardner explains that intelligence is not a single entity that can be measured using a simple IQ test, but that people are born with a number of intelligences of varying strengths and constraints. He suggests that these intelligences do not work independently, but complement each other and work interdependently.

In his book *Frames of Mind*[3] Gardner outlines seven intelligences:

- *Linguistic intelligence* – being word smart
- *Logical–mathematical intelligence* – being number smart
- *Musical intelligence* – being musically smart
- *Bodily–kinaesthetic intelligence* – being body smart
- *Spatial intelligence* – being picture smart
- *Interpersonal intelligence* – being people smart
- *Intrapersonal intelligence* – being myself smart.

Gardner did not see this list as being exhaustive. He suggests: 'there will never be a master list of three, seven or three hundred that can be endorsed by all investigators.'[4] Other

---

3 Howard Gardner, *Frames of Mind, The Theory of Multiple Intelligences,* 1983, p77–292
4 ibid, p64

forms of intelligence have been considered for inclusion including: naturalist intelligence; spiritual intelligence; existential intelligence; moral intelligence.

The challenge we face is how to respond to the wide range of intelligences that people show. How do we value and use the broad range of ways in which people are smart? Could our communities be better at matching intelligences to roles and to opportunities for service in the church? How do we identify the interpersonal intelligence of our members and offer them opportunities for evangelism and pastoring? Do we provide space and time for linguistically intelligent individuals to respond in church through song writing and poetry? How would we support an individual with a logical–mathematical intelligence to explore Scripture in ways that are meaningful to them? How can we enable individuals, demonstrating such a wide range of intelligences, to thrive and to feel entirely included?

Challenge 3: We are different in personality

Story

Nina says, 'When I was a child I loved church. I loved listening to stories and joining in with the songs that were sung. I loved seeing the colours of the seasons reflected in my church and the patterns represented in the church year. I didn't enjoy Sunday school as much. My Sunday school teachers were always really worried that I wasn't enjoying it because I didn't tell them or show them. I hated being in a small group and I didn't like being asked questions – especially when I didn't have time to think about the answers. At the age of 12 I decided that I wasn't going to join the youth programme. Even now I would not consider going to a house group or Bible study in my church. When I have tried to be part of a small group others think I am aloof or feel anxious because I haven't shared an answer.'

Nina is not unusual; her introvert personality means she is part of a group that makes up 25 per cent[5] of society. Nina struggles to feel included as others see her personality type as unusual, and do not understand how she can function best with others.

There are differing theories around introversion and extroversion, but the most popular thinking is found in the work of Carl Jung. Jung[6] proposes that our introversion and extroversion are a single continuous dimension of our personality – a continuum. It is recognised that individuals fluctuate in their own behaviours. Even extreme introverts or extroverts do not always act according to their 'type'.

Those who demonstrate an extroverted personality:

- are energised by being around people
- are seen as sociable, outgoing and socially adept
- tend to demonstrate gregariousness
- might have the ability to think as they talk.

Those who demonstrate an introverted personality:

- are energised by being alone
- tend to enjoy thinking and reflecting before talking
- might avoid social situations
- desire time alone after being in a social context
- might be misconstrued as being shy.

5 Marti Olsen Laney, *The Introvert Advantage: How to Thrive in an Extrovert World*, Workman, 2002, p15
6 Carl Jung, *Psychological Types (Collected Works of CG Jung)*, Routledge, 1992

Those who demonstrate an ambiverted personality:

- find that their behaviours fall centrally between extrovert and introvert
- are moderately comfortable with groups and social situations
- relish time alone from the crowds.

As a church community, how do we foster and nurture spiritual growth in individuals like Nina? How can we support those who lead and are part of small groups who do not yet recognise the needs of Nina and introverts like her?

Challenge 4: We are at different stages of our faith development

The Sunday all-age context can certainly feel like a Christmas dining experience that is a disaster waiting to happen!

In one service you might be trying to meet the needs of those who are visiting church and have no faith or are anti-faith, alongside those who come and attend because their husband or wife makes them. You might also be trying to grow the faith of those who have had faith for many decades, individuals who have nagging doubts or are seeking and questioning. Then there are others who are at a stage in their faith where experience and emotion create a feeling of belonging. These people might express frustration that the church context is not 'powerful', 'hard-hitting' or 'emotionally gripping'.

The challenge of meeting the needs of all those individuals, who are at such very different stages of their faith development, is a very real one.

Westerhoff

John Westerhoff explains that, 'if we take seriously the styles of faith and faith's expansion, we must conclude that no single educational program for any age-group is valid.'[7] Westerhoff's thinking around the development of faith is widely known and respected. He argues that faith development cannot be purely tied to age. Using the growing rings of a tree as a symbol, he outlines four styles and characteristics of the faith pilgrimage. His book likens the development of these styles to the growth of a tree where new rings encompass the existing one – not replacing them or rejecting them but incorporating them. These four stages are found in Westerhoff's work *Will our Children have Faith?*.

Experienced faith

An experienced faith is one that is based on an experience of faith that is lived out. Westerhoff explains, 'no one can determine another's faith and no one can give another faith, but we can be faithful and share our life and our faith with another. Others, regardless of age, can do the same with us, and through this sharing we sustain, transmit and expand our faith.'[8] In children this experienced faith is characterised by mimicking, recreating, imagining and exploring the faith that they can see, hear, touch, taste and smell. Adults who are new to faith begin their faith journey by observing, listening, engaging and making their own responses.

Affiliative faith

Westerhoff sees affiliation as an essential stage in faith expansion. Individuals reach out with a desire to be connected to others, to be known, useful and accepted.

---

7 John Westerhoff, *Will Our Children Have Faith?*, Morehouse Publishing, 3rd edn, 2012, p99
8 ibid, p91

The authority that comes from owning a shared story is an essential element to this affiliation, according to Westerhoff. Hearing, rehearing and owning our shared story, experiencing it in images and words, are important aspects of our sense of belonging.

Westerhoff goes on to warn that it would be easy to think that faith is about knowledge, but that there needs to be a strong emotional connection. He makes an argument that activities such as music, drama, storytelling and other art forms are pivotal for developing emotional aspects of faith. He says that, 'actions in the realms of the affections are prior to acts of thinking ... Opportunities for experiencing awe, wonder and mystery ... are needed by us all.'[9]

Searching faith

Westerhoff sees an expansion of faith from an affiliative style to a searching style as being demonstrated in three behaviours.

First, you would expect to see doubt and critical judgement. An individual at this stage is looking to verify and validate their understanding of faith. Secondly, you would expect to see experimentation. An individual might test their faith by comparing it to that of others, questioning their different traditions.

It is only after this challenging and awkward phase that a person has developed their own faith identity, along with deep convictions and beliefs. Only then will an individual demonstrate the third behaviour of a searching faith, 'a commitment' that leads to an owned faith.

Owned faith

John Westerhoff emphasises that an owned faith 'is what

9 ibid, p95

historically has been called "conversion". Conversion experiences may be sudden or gradual, dramatic or undramatic, emotional or intellectual, but they always involve a major change in a person's thinking, feeling and willing – in short, their total behaviour.'[10]

Westerhoff outlines the challenges faced by having different people at different stages of faith together. He argues that very few adults have an owned faith, and that many adults maintain a faith that is affiliated. He explains his belief that 'in every church ... a variety of education environments and experiences that make possible the expansion of faith, is needed.'[11]

Westerhoff argues that finding ways of being together will enable individuals to move from one stage of faith to another. He expounds the idea that we are encouraged to expand our faith and enter a new stage of faith when one or more of the following happen:[12]

- We experience the expanded faith (at a different faith stage) of a role model.
- We find ourselves in a situation 'we cannot resolve satisfactorily through actions consistent with our present style of faith'.
- We pass through relevant and appropriate rites of passage in our faith community.

Fowler
James Fowler offers a different approach to faith development. However, his thinking reflects the same issues when addressing the needs of the individuals who are at such different stages of

10 ibid, p97
11 ibid, p99
12 James Fowler, *Stages of Faith: The Psychology of Human Development and the Quest for Meaning*, Harper & Row, 1981, p100

their faith. Fowler proposes six stages of faith in *Stages of Faith: The Psychology of Human Development and the Quest for Meaning*. These stages are primarily about the development of faith from childhood to adulthood.[13]

Infancy – Undifferentiated faith
* In infancy our primal understanding of love, hope, trust are formed through our relationship with our parents or primary carers.
* Development of language indicates a movement to stage 1.

Stage 1 – Intuitive–projective faith
* *Makes sense of faith:* using concrete examples and experiences.
* *Has faith shaped by:* caring adults who provide the concrete experiences.
* *Stage of faith is characterised by:* imaginative mind of the child mixing fantasy with reality.

Stage 2 – Mythic–literal faith
* *Makes sense of faith:* through sense experience. Children are looking for proofs of the facts.
* *Has faith shaped by:* parent viewpoint, along with a growing impact from others outside the family (teacher, friends, wider family).
* *Stage of faith is characterised by:* the sorting of facts from fantasy.

Stage 3 – Synthetic–conventional faith
* *Makes sense of faith:* through a developing personality, feelings and anxieties.
* *Has faith shaped by:* others – this is more often through friends, school and eventually work.

---

13 ibid, p119–199

- *Stage of faith is characterised by:* connecting experiences and comparing experiences with others.

Stage 4 – Individuative–reflective faith
- *Makes sense of faith:* personally and reflectively.
- *Has faith shaped by:* a strong sense of personal responsibility for own beliefs and faith.
- *Stage of faith is characterised by:* complex tensions between the beliefs of groups they belong to and their own strongly held values.

Stage 5 – Conjunctive faith
- *Makes sense of faith:* while deepening a personal awareness of own prejudices, feelings and experiences.
- *Has faith shaped by:* a range of differing viewpoints.
- *Stage of faith is characterised by:* an openness to symbols, myths and rituals.

Stage 6 – Universalised faith
- Has made sense of faith.
- *Stage of faith is characterised by:* costly sacrificial social justice and a depth of love and concern for others – this stage is not often reached.

Fowler's faith development theory is a challenge in both an all-age context where people of different ages need to have faith shaped in different ways to enable them to develop, and also a challenge in the segregated contexts in which we function. Our youth groups and adult Bible studies are filled with people who demonstrate faith at a range of stages.

Is it possible to create more open-ended opportunities for faith development, where an individual can give voice to their faith, and have faith shaped at the stage where they find themself?

Explore Together

The Christmas meal metaphor at the beginning of this chapter perhaps over eggs the challenges of being together. However, the value of such a meal is clear. Being together as a faith community – represented in a rich variety of ages, experiences, spiritual styles, stages of development and personality types – presents a huge challenge. However, the value of this is also very clear. Like the family Christmas meal, at its heart stands the very act of sharing with one another, growing love for each other, passing on traditions, hearing the family story and experiencing a deep sense of belonging. Such an occasion is powerful, meaningful and significant. So, how can such an experience be facilitated?

Explore Together is an approach that seeks to address the challenges of being together. Big questions are posed around a passage of Scripture, and then individuals listen to God, responding in a range of explore zones, before sharing their responses and answers with others in a small group.

The explore zones (further explained in Chapters 4 and 5) give permission for individuals to explore and express faith using their own spiritual style, personal intelligence or preference for learning. The family member who has a preference for learning visually, or who has a symbol-centred spirituality, might decide to explore the questions in the colour zone. The individual with an extrovert personality or with an inter-personal intelligence might choose to talk through their answers in the chat zone. The beauty of this is that, as individuals, we are exploring in a personal and meaningful way, but sharing our responses so that we are shaping and being shaped by the community of faith around us.

Sharing in small groups is a key element of Explore Together. It enables those who prefer to listen to be soaked in the experiences and ideas of those who do not mind talking and sharing their thoughts. Within the community of faith who are exploring together you are likely to find representatives of the various stages of faith. While sharing their responses they have the opportunity to influence once another, to feel that as individuals they belong and to see themselves as active participants in building their faith.

Story

Nine-year-old Freya modelled brilliantly the response of an active participant able to powerfully shape the faith of those around her. As an individual with a word-centred spirituality she spent time in the word zone as she was exploring.

She came out of that time with a prayer that she had written. It was an expression of faith that was deeply personal but shaped the faith of all around:

With a foundation of faith I will stay strong
With your love I shall never fail
If I stay by your side I shall always be safe
If I walk with you your love is an anchor to save me from my sin
From a world of darkness you shine so brightly
From the heavens you gleam
I turn my back, you love me still
I crouch from sorrow, you hold me close
From the shadow of sin, you welcome me in.

Explore Together meets head on the challenges of being together with a range of personal learning preferences, spiritual styles and intelligences. It enables individuals who are at different stages of faith to operate at a level appropriate for them, and to shape the journey of faith that others are travelling.

Explore Together is a very pragmatic response to all of the challenges posed but, as Chapter 3 argues, it also fits tightly with a biblical precedent for growing faith together.

Reflect

If you would find it helpful, use the following questions and writing spaces to reflect on the ideas in this chapter.

1   Why is coming together as whole church/community so often a challenge? Which three of the following words best describe your all together times? Which word(s) best describe how you would like these times to be?

joyful	exciting
celebration	irritation
unhappy	authentic
chaos	fruitful

2   How do you feel about Csinos' spiritual styles? Which style do you identify with the most? Does your church/community favour a particular style above the others?

3   How does your church/community help people to discover their preferred spiritual style? How might they be able to do this more effectively?

4   Do you prefer Fleming's VARK model of learning styles or Gardner's theory of multiple intelligences? Why?

5   Could your church/community be better at matching learning styles/intelligences to roles and opportunities for service? How might you go about this?

6   Are you an introvert or an extrovert? Does your church/community demonstrate equal value for both of these personality types? What more could be done to make sure that both introverts and extroverts feel equally valued, respected and involved in your church/community?

7   How does your church/community ensure that people at all stages of faith development are welcome?

Chapter 3

Exploring together

If we are to ensure that the challenges of being together (as outlined in Chapter 2) do not become an obstacle, and if we need to dispel the fears attached to coming together as a whole church around God's Word, we need to become confident in our conviction that exploring together is not just beneficial, but necessary.

Keith White, in his book *The Growth of Love*, outlines five elements that need to exist for a child's development, which therefore have implications for 'good-enough' parenting. He asserts that community is one of these five elements. White's view is that one such function of the church is to act as a microcosm of community, bridging the lives of children and families with the community at large. He suggests that church, 'will want to model a variety of relationships in society' and that this will be evident in 'shared meals, shared worship, shared learning, shared decision making, shared helping in the community and shared engagement in global mission' as opposed to routinely choosing 'to split the family by age, so that its members find themselves separated by much of the worship and other activities.'[1]

---

1 Keith White, *The Growth of Love*, 2008, p128

Dr Kara Powell outlines the necessity of 'sticky relationships' for making faith last.[2] As a response to research by the Fuller Institute, which outlines essential elements for continued and maturing faith, she argues, 'in an effort to offer relevant and developmentally appropriate teaching and fellowship for children and teenagers, we have segregated – and I use the term intentionally and not lightly – kids from the rest of the church. And that segregation is causing kids to shelve their faith.' Powell upholds the view that children and young people who have a network and web of relationships with others of all ages are likely to grow in faith and stick with it.

It is clear from both White's and Powell's work, and a plethora of other research being generated, that being together is not only hugely advantageous but essential for children and young people.

But, what does the Bible itself have to say about the necessity of exploring together as a community? Why is exploring together so potent and significant?

The significance of hearing from God

Paul reminds us that, 'All Scripture is God-breathed' (2 Timothy 3:16). In Genesis we see God breathing life into the first man, Adam (2:7). As we share in the Bible together we are engaging with words and meaning that are loaded with the very life-giving breath of God. As we read from the Word together and are caused to listen, reflect, be moved and challenged, we are drawn so close to God it is as if we can feel his breath on our faces. We are changed by what God has to say to us, we carry God's 'breath' and we become the 'Word' of God to each other.

---

2 Kara Powell & Chap Clark, *Sticky Faith*, Zondervan, 2011, p95

Our words, interactions, thoughts and behaviours have the potential to be a breath of fresh air to those we meet both in the church and out of it. Being immersed in the Bible is deeply personal, but also becomes deeply communal.

When we experience God through his Word there is an overflowing impact on others. This impact is not accidental. Others capture a glimpse of who God is and what he is saying. God's Word is therefore spoken to us and his Word is spoken through us.

Evidence of this exists throughout the Bible. One such example is found in Genesis, where the Word of God is spoken to Abraham and he receives the promise of a descendant.

> *I will surely bless you and make your descendants as numerous as the stars in the sky and as the sand on the seashore. Your descendants will take possession of the cities of their enemies, and through your offspring all nations on earth will be blessed, because you have obeyed me.*
>
> *Genesis 22:17,18*

This clearly is the promise of children to Abraham, and also the promise of Jesus to the world through Abraham. Abraham was blessed to be a blessing. He heard God, and as a result we have seen and heard God in the person of Jesus.

Hearing from God, developing a new insight and being in a place to express it with immediacy is powerful. Not only do we share the excitement of that moment, we can be challenged together by what God is saying and become accountable to one another for making God's challenge or Word a reality in our everyday lives. When we hear from God it has an impact on others around us.

A church was exploring together Psalm 46:

¹ *God is our refuge and strength,*
  an ever-present help in trouble.
² *Therefore we will not fear, though the earth give way*
  and the mountains fall into the heart of the sea,
³ *though its waters roar and foam*
  and the mountains quake with their surging.
⁴ *There is a river whose streams make glad the city of God,*
  the holy place where the Most High dwells.
⁵ *God is within her, she will not fall;*
  God will help her at break of day.
⁶ *Nations are in uproar, kingdoms fall;*
  he lifts his voice, the earth melts.
⁷ *The Lord Almighty is with us;*
  the God of Jacob is our fortress.
⁸ *Come and see what the Lord has done,*
  the desolations he has brought on the earth.
⁹ *He makes wars cease*
  to the ends of the earth.
  He breaks the bow and shatters the spear;
  he burns the shields with fire.
¹⁰ *He says, "Be still, and know that I am God;*
  I will be exalted among the nations,
  I will be exalted in the earth."
¹¹ *The Lord Almighty is with us;*
  the God of Jacob is our fortress.

Psalm 46

One of the questions being explored was: 'What is the point of praise?'

Ten-year-old Maeve shared excitedly that she had found an answer. She shared that 'praise is gigantic'. She explained that praise must be bigger than her, because it was about God who can stop whole countries from fighting one another.

One of the adults in the group, Simon, was visibly moved. He explained that he had found it hard to praise God in his life, because life was difficult for him, and he had decided that praise was pointless because he didn't have something to praise God for. He shared that if praise is bigger than him and his situation, he needed to find a way to praise again.

Maeve left church that day knowing that God had spoken to her, and Simon felt that God had challenged him. Intentionally sharing the Bible together places us in a prime position for receiving, seeing and sharing what God is doing and saying.

Hebrews tells us, 'the word of God is alive and active. Sharper than any double-edged sword, it penetrates even to dividing soul and spirit, joints and marrow; it judges the thoughts and attitudes of the heart' (4:12). As we look into the Bible we can hear from God. What we hear penetrates our thoughts and attitudes. It has the potential to challenge our being and doing, and brings about transformation. When we look into the Bible together we potentially surround ourselves with those who are being transformed, and in ourselves become an example and model of what God is doing. Sharing the Bible together can arguably be a catalyst for transformation, as Joe's story explains:

Story

Joe's story: 8-year-old Joe had been listening to his minister talk about the fact that when we help others, it is as if we are doing it for Jesus. Joe had looked into the Bible himself, reading and re-reading Matthew 25:37–40.

'Then the righteous will answer him, "Lord, when did we see you hungry and feed you, or thirsty and give you something to drink? When did we see you a stranger and invite you in, or needing clothes and clothe you? When did we see you ill or in prison and go to visit you?"
'The King will reply, "Truly I tell you, whatever you did for one of the least of these brothers and sisters of mine, you did for me."'

After the service the church shared in a big lunch. Joe had noticed the man sitting outside church, homeless and hungry, who would not accept the invitation of eating with everyone else. Joe took his lunch outside and gave it to the man sitting there. You can imagine the impact this had on the adults and church community. Sunday lunches in church have not been the same since. Lots more individuals have been invited to attend, and food is taken to those who could not or would not come.

The significance of learning from each other

If we accept the premise that God's Word is spoken to us and that his Word is spoken through us, then our interdependency is already clear. In Hebrews 10:24 we read:

And let us consider how we may spur one another on towards love and good deeds, not giving up meeting together, as some are in the habit of doing, but encouraging one another – and all the more as you see the Day approaching.

Throughout the Bible, God's people are encouraged to gather and learn from each other. In the Old Testament they were encouraged to assemble and learn the Law. In Deuteronomy we read:

> 'Assemble the people – men, women and children, and the foreigners residing in your towns – so that they can listen and learn to fear the Lord your God and follow carefully all the words of this law' (31:12).

These passages teach us the value of learning within a community that is both diverse and inclusive of age, gender and culture. In doing so we can learn the Law, 'spur each other on' and 'encourage one another'.

In his Gospel, Luke tells of the 12-year-old Jesus who, instead of returning home with his parents, remains in the Temple. When Jesus' parents notice he is missing they panic, run back to the Temple and find Jesus with the teachers. He is 'listening to them and asking them questions' (Luke 2:46).

Luke informs us that Jesus was listening and questioning, but he goes on to say, 'Everyone who heard him was amazed at his understanding and his answers' (Luke 2:47). What a powerful picture of God himself listening and asking questions! When I read that passage of Scripture I do find myself wondering who learnt the most in that interaction.

Jesus himself makes it clear that children have something valuable to teach us – this is apparent even without the advantage of them 'being God'.

Having spent a period of time in towns that had rejected his teaching, miracles and ministry, Jesus prays and says, 'I praise you, Father, Lord of heaven and earth, because you have hidden these things from the wise and learned, and revealed them to little children' (Matthew 11:25).

Later in that same Gospel Jesus is challenged to respond to a discussion that his disciples are having about who is the greatest in the kingdom of heaven. Jesus' response is to call a child to stand among them; he then says, 'unless you change and become like little children, you will never enter the kingdom of heaven ... whoever welcomes one such child in my name welcomes me' (Matthew 18:1–5).

What is happening here is of significance.

If we can assume that Jesus is teaching sat down (as recorded in Mark's telling of this story (Mark 9:35) and knowing that it was tradition for rabbis to stand to read the scripture and sit to teach), calling a child to stand among them would have caused the disciples to physically look up to the child, powerfully re-emphasising the need to do so spiritually.

He is also making it clear that the very presence of the child has something precious to teach about the values of the kingdom.

Story

Tom's story: Having listened to Luke's Bible passage outlining the resurrection of Jesus, 10-year-old Tom went away to explore with the question: 'What have you learned about this story that you didn't know before?'

Tom shared his response with all those present: 'When I was in year 4 (aged 8 years) I knew that I couldn't see very well, everything was blurry. I didn't want to tell anyone because I was afraid that I would need to wear glasses. I thought that they wouldn't look cool and that people would laugh at me. My mum took me to the optician when I went into year 6 because my eyes had got really bad. I did have to wear glasses. The story today has made me think about my eyes. Before I had glasses I couldn't see very well but as soon as I put my glasses on I could see clearly. Knowing about what Jesus did for me is just like that; before I really understood it properly it was like not being able to see clearly but now I know, everything makes sense. I don't care if people laugh at me because I know the truth; I can see clearly.'

The adults around were amazed at the understanding Tom showed. Tom had taught something very precious to those who were older and younger on that day.

When we look to society as a whole, where do we find diverse and inclusive gatherings of people who intentionally set out to learn from each other? When we look outwardly into our communities and inwardly to our churches, where can we find opportunities for us to learn from all ages? In our age-segregated churches, where are the opportunities we have to learn from children or young people?

Story

Anna's story: On one Sunday after church I was talking to a member of the congregation called Anna. During the growth of the church there had been an influx of young families. Anna struggled with the noise that children were making during the service, and strongly disliked the fact children could walk freely around during times of worship.

One particular Sunday, Anna came to speak to me, with tears in her eyes. She had seen two young children playing; in the course of their playing one had intentionally hurt the other. After a moment of sadness despite being hurt, the offended child turned to the other giving both a toy and a hug to them. This simple act had provided Anna with a glimpse of God's grace and taught her something that would make a deep impression on her understanding of God.

The significance of questions

In 2013 the *Daily Telegraph* reported on a study that claimed British mothers are asked on average 300 questions a day. This equated to more questions every hour than a teacher or doctor. The report also suggested that 'girls aged four are most curious, asking on average 390 questions each day – averaging a question every 1 minute 56 seconds of their waking day.'[3]

It should not be a surprise to us that the individuals who are at the peak of learning and development should be the ones seeking answers to the most questions. Questions allow children to make sense of the world, think critically and consider the complexities of life. Asking and answering questions is a dominant feature of places where learning happens intentionally. Asking and answering questions is a defining feature of pre-schools, primary schools, colleges and businesses. Where do we find opportunity to ask and answer questions in church communities?

Jesus asked questions
It was to two blind men sitting on the roadside that Jesus asked, 'What do you want me to do for you?' (Matthew 20:32). To his

---

3 The *Daily Telegraph*, 28 March 2013, 'Mothers asked nearly 300 questions a day'

disciples Jesus asked, 'Who do people say the Son of Man is?' (Matthew 16:13) and then goes further to ask the question: 'Who do you say I am?' (Matthew 16:15). To the teachers and Pharisees Jesus asked, 'Why are you thinking these things in your hearts?' (Luke 5:22). In his teaching he asked, 'If [salt] loses its saltiness, how can it be made salty again?' (Luke 14:34) and 'Can any one of you by worrying add a single hour to your life?' (Matthew 6:27).

On meeting Mary after his resurrection he asked, 'Woman, why are you crying? Who is it you are looking for?' (John 20:15).

These are just a sample of Jesus' questions. Asking questions was a significant part of his teaching ministry. It was not that Jesus did not know the answers to the questions, but just that in posing them he was offering something powerful to the person being questioned.

In asking questions Jesus deeply involved, and personally challenged, those who were learning from him. The questions he asked skilfully carved out a depth of understanding that would not have been developed had he just spoken the information to those listening.

Jesus answered questions

Nicodemus came to Jesus at night. Despite being a Pharisee and teacher of the Law he found himself asking questions of Jesus. In response to Jesus' teaching about being born again he asked, 'How can someone be born when they are old?' (John 3:4); 'How can this be?' (John 3:9).

The rich young ruler came to Jesus and asked, 'What must I do to inherit eternal life?' (Mark 10:17). On occasions, Jesus answered questions with more questions. For example, after healing a man who could not walk and forgiving his sins:

...some teachers of the law were sitting there, thinking to themselves, 'Why does this fellow talk like that? He's blaspheming! Who can forgive sins but God alone?' Immediately Jesus knew in his spirit that this was what they were thinking in their hearts, and he said to them, 'Why are you thinking these things? Which is easier: to say to this paralysed man, "Your sins are forgiven," or to say, "Get up, take your mat and walk"?'

Mark 2:6–9

People came to Jesus with their questions because he had the authority and knowledge to answer them. In responding to the questions of individuals, he could meet their deepest needs.

The significance of questions is apparent in the Alpha courses that have been running in many churches. According to an article in *The Independent*,[4] 1.2 million Britons have attended an Alpha course. Adverts for Alpha have been displayed on buses and billboards across the UK. Often these adverts use a question mark as a logo. The advertisements have asked, 'Got questions about life?', 'Does God exist?', 'Is this it?', 'Where am I going?'.

Each Alpha session takes a question as its theme, and allows individuals the opportunity to ask questions of their own. But, why should questions just be the preserve of those who are not part of the church yet? Does our need to know and understand end when we become committed followers of Jesus?

Where can we facilitate opportunities for all ages in our communities to ask openly and honestly their own deepest questions? How do we help each other ask questions of Jesus

---

4 *The Independent*, 31 March 2013, 'Inside the Alpha Course – British Christianity's Biggest Success Story'

so that our deepest needs are met?

Carl's story: In conversation with 23-year-old Carl, he explained that his lifetime of church experience drove him away from Jesus. He was tired of pretending to believe what he was told he had to believe, and felt that he could not ask the honest questions that he had. It was in what he describes as 'the wilderness alone' that he really experienced Jesus.

Carl explained his viewpoint: 'Religion was found in the church. For me church was full of man-made junk, and little of Jesus. I wanted Jesus, and thankfully I eventually found him.' Carl eventually found his way to belonging to a church small group where he now feels able to share his doubts, ask questions and challenge the answers others share.

Moving forward

The challenges of being together and the biblical precedence for growing faith together cause us to look for ground to move forward. An expedition of this kind requires us to forge a path to enable us to journey together.

As highlighted in Chapter 1, we are a pick and mix society that has become more and more accustomed to choice. We have information at our fingertips and we are conditioned and equipped to tailor our experiences to reflect our own preferences. Within our faith communities the younger generations are educated and encouraged to be active learners: to seek out information, ask questions and find answers.

Explore Together places the Bible at the centre of all of this diversity and releases the community to explore its message and hear God's voice in a way that embraces their natural preferences. It encourages the community to come together to share their thoughts, questions and revelations with each other: the elderly with the young, the new believer with the mature traveller, the learned scholar with the inquisitive toddler.

At the heart of Explore Together a passage from the Bible is shared, open questions are posed for the community to explore and a variety of zones are made available where they can engage and grapple with the questions and ultimately hear from God. The community are then brought together to share what they have discovered or created.

Story

Martin's story: Explore Together enabled a lively community church to engage with the Bible in a fresh way. Those who took part felt that it provided them with a way to be more open to God's specific revelation through the Bible.

Martin was one of the leaders in the chat zone. Among the group was a man who was attending this church for the first time; he shared that he was exploring the Christian and other faiths. The group read through the Bible passage and then shared with each other through the questions that had been posed how it had impacted them. The man was intrigued by some of the comments that were raised in the discussion, and asked some of his own questions, which the group answered as best they could.

Says Martin: 'I really felt that God was meeting this guy where he was at and was involving us in the process! It struck me that the opportunities to ask questions in the way he did are few and far between in a 'usual' church service. He was new to the church and wasn't part of a small group (the normal setting for this type of Bible exploration), and I don't think he would have felt comfortable going up to a stranger in the church to ask his questions.'

Story

Steve's story: It was with some trepidation and lots of prayer that Steve dared to attempt Explore Together in a traditional church setting, on a Sunday.

With about 140 to 150 people ranging in age from babies to 90+, the all-together service was replaced with Explore Together. Steve got lots of great feedback, with several older members of the congregation saying how good it was to be able to share and hear other people's input. Steve even had someone phone him after the service to say how they loved it. An enthusiastic teacher said it was just how they learn at school, and one elder suggested that Explore Together could be used for all their all-together (family) services.

But it wasn't just the children and older members who found Explore Together rewarding. The youth pastor thought it was great and worked for the young people who attended. One of the young people even posted the results of their exploration in the busy zone on Facebook. Not only were they exploring the Bible together at the church but also with their Facebook friends.

Overall, what particularly delighted Steve was the level of participation and how much people did things together in the zones.

Explore Together 'works' because it puts into practice all of the theoretical learning we have access to. It makes provision for learning preferences, spiritual styles, faith formation and personality types. It draws from our understanding of biblical community and gives a place and a voice to all of its members, from the youngest to the oldest. It creates intentional space to hear from God and recognises the value, impact and importance of learning from each other, opening up opportunities for dialogue and storytelling across generations.

Explore Together is more than just another all-age resource – it is a tool that can aid progressive thinking about discipleship, pastoral care, being community and Bible engagement, and can be used in any setting where Bible engagement is the focus. Exploring together breaks down barriers and bravely surrenders control to the Holy Spirit.

Reflect

If you would find it helpful, use the following questions and writing spaces to reflect on the ideas in this chapter.

1   Why is coming together as a whole church/community so important?

2   Everyone has the potential to contribute something of value, no matter their age, stage of faith development, personality or preferred learning style. Do you agree with this statement? Why, or why not? How do you feel about adults learning from the children in your church/community – as opposed to children learning from adults?

3   What can you learn from Tom's story? How might this impact your practice?

4   Does your church/community give opportunity for people at ask and answer difficult questions? How might this be encouraged?

5   How might you create intentional space to hear from God in your church/community gatherings?

6   How do you feel about surrendering control to the Holy Spirit as you explore the Bible together with your church/community? Why?

Chapter 4

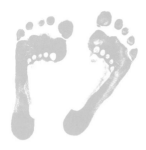

The benefits of exploring together

I'm actually a little bit ashamed to admit this in print but I do so knowing with confidence that I am not alone in my confession. Well, here goes: *Sometimes, not always, I will choose to go and listen to someone speak just because I like them or their style*.

This is particularly true when I am ticking through the seminar brochures at Christian conferences. If my favourite speakers are listed I'll probably include them in my timetable, whatever the subject of their seminar. Adversely, I will also opt not to go to something if I don't like the style of the speaker.

This is where the confession gets a bit more brutal: *I have done this at a local level too!!* There, I've said it. It's out there now. I, Lianne Semans Smith, am a person who is guilty of deciding whether or not to go to a service based on who is preaching that day. While I'm on a confessional roll I'm also going to own up to being a sermon critic. Again, I do this in the knowledge that I'm not on my own.

Sometimes the Bible message gets lost in the personality, style and ability of whoever is delivering it. In Chapter 1 we highlighted that a biblical community needs to be focused on God; my confessions are an example of what can happen when our focus shifts from God to us. Many of us are guilty of allowing our own likes and dislikes to get in the way of worship. When we focus on who is delivering the message rather than whose message they are delivering, barriers are created that can prevent us from hearing from God.

The predominant and preferred method of Bible teaching within faith communities is through an appointed teacher or preacher. The preacher interprets the scripture for us, and we listen. This is indeed one of the ways that God communicates with his people. There are many examples of this in the Bible, where God appoints a spokesperson to deliver his message. God appointed Moses to lead his people and gave him the authority to speak on his behalf to the nation of Israel. Elijah was one of the many prophets to whom God spoke directly with words of warning, instruction and encouragement for him to pass on to others.

Jesus himself modelled this method of teaching. The Sermon on the Mount, for example, was delivered by Jesus to crowds of people who were hanging on his every word.

Teaching and prophecy are listed as spiritual gifts and, indisputably, have a very significant place within a biblical community. However, God does not restrict his communication methods to certain learned individuals, he speaks in many and varied ways to individuals and whole nations. He speaks through visions and dreams, angels and creation, stories and testimonies, prophecy and supernatural encounters and, sometimes, in his own audible voice. Jesus did not restrict his teaching methods to preaching sermons. Eugene Peterson's translation of Matthew 11:29 concisely describes how Jesus helped his disciples to form their faith: 'Walk with me and work with me – watch how I do it. Learn the unforced rhythms of grace.

I won't lay anything heavy or ill-fitting on you' (The Message). Jesus had his disciples get actively involved in their learning: they listened to his conversations; they saw how he dealt with every situation; they witnessed the relationship he had with his Father; they asked him questions; he asked them questions; he encouraged them to speak and listen directly to God. The disciples weren't taught their faith, they caught it.

On the occasions when we come together to worship and learn we are sometimes guilty of restricting these creative and exciting encounters by prescribing how and when they are going to take place.

A walk in the park

When my children were small we went on a family outing to the Botanic Gardens in Southport; my brother and his son and our parents came too. It was a really pleasant experience.

We entered the gate and were greeted with signposts that directed us to all of the beautiful sections of this well maintained park. The pathways were all even and tidy, which made pushing my toddler's buggy really easy. We visited the aviary, where the birds fluttered and perched around their netted enclosure; there was the Victorian fernery, a large glass conservatory which was home to an amazing collection of large-leafed plants and little quirky statues; and my mum was wowed by the beautiful floral displays situated around the park, each showcasing carefully selected seasonal blooms in co-ordinated colours and shapes.

The children were free to trot along the pathways – they knew to keep off the grass where the signs requested them to do so. There were lots of comfy benches where my parents could sit and watch us while we played crazy golf under the branches of the huge trees carefully selected decades ago to enhance and define the parameter of the park. The quaint tea rooms provided us with warm respite from the intermittent showers of rain and the ice cream parlour gave us a bargaining tool when the children started to show signs of boredom.

It was beautiful, neat and tidy, it was safe. We were treated to the sights, sounds and smells of creation. We had to keep to the paths, we weren't allowed to touch the flowers or climb the trees but we had everything we needed to enjoy our time there. The park planners and gardeners had chosen well for us and we went home content.

Our church services can be very much like a walk in the park. They are organised, safe and comfortable. Teams of people decide how we are going to learn and worship when we meet together. They are like the park planners and gardeners. There are plans for what songs will be sung, what prayers will be prayed, what Bible passage will be shared and how it will be interpreted. Our children's and youth groups are planned and delivered. Then, when it is all over, we get to relax with a tea or coffee and a biscuit. We know exactly what to expect and when everything happens. Like our family trip to the Botanic Gardens, these times can be great. We have a pleasant experience and we get to encounter something of God through the process.

Explore Together enhances this experience by transforming a walk in the park to a forest adventure.

A forest adventure

As one member of our family is of the four-legged variety our regular outings tend to be to local forests. Our dog does not cope well on a lead and most maintained parks make that a requirement. The forests we visited when the children were young were less restricted; our dog, the children and I were free to forage and explore. There were no official pathways, only those worn by the footsteps of those who had gone before us. The uneven terrain made trips and stumbles commonplace. It was a place of hand holding, piggybacks and carries as pushing a pram was impossible. The words, 'mummy help me' were called out frequently as the children climbed in and out of exciting situations.

The forests were full of surprises and hidden treasures. Interesting shaped branches, random patches of pretty flowers and toadstools, colonies of writhing insects and creatures hiding under dying logs, stagnant pools of water inviting wellie-clad feet to wade through. I remember our children searching for the best digging sticks so that they could scrape down through the soil into the clay to make models.

An endless barrage of questions and conversations filled our forest adventures, 'mummy look', 'what is this?', 'how did that get there?', 'can I eat this?', 'what's that smell?'. We built dens, made up stories, played hide and seek, got very dirty and sometimes lost. One moment we would be basking in sunlight and the next we would be in darkness under a ceiling of dense branches feeling a little scared. Every time we left the forest we would be carrying little bags (dog owners always carry little bags!) filled with forest treasures which remained in our home for weeks, sometimes months, to remind us of our adventures. In fact, my daughter is now at university and on a shelf in her bedroom at home sits a little forest man made out of the clay that she dug up with her digging stick when she was 7 years old.

No two trips to the forest were ever the same. Each time we chose to take alternative routes, discovered new treasures and encountered awe-inspiring surprises. We really had no other expectation than to explore.

When a community explore together they encounter opportunities to engage with the Bible in the same way that my little family encountered opportunities during their forest adventures.

We were all in the same place at the same time, encountering the same trees and pathways, pools and mud pits, creatures and smells, but we were free to discover and explore the delights of the forest in our own way. I was happy to meander around the pathways, keeping a watchful eye on our children while I absorbed with all of my senses the beauty of the overall scene and marvelled in the intricate complexities of nature. Occasionally I pointed out things that I thought warranted my children's attention; the little things that they might miss in their eagerness to be everywhere all at once.

Our daughter would be busy, touching, foraging, digging and collecting objects of interest which could come in useful later. Her endless questions guided us into deep family conversations about all sorts of subjects. Our son discovered routes up, down and around obstacles that we would probably never have noticed had we been there without him.

Our forest adventures taught me so much about our children's likes, dislikes, fears and interests. Each of us came away from these experiences richer in our knowledge of each other and the forest. Our encounter would have been very different if we had taken our children by the hand and decided for them how they would spend their time on the basis of what we wanted them to experience and know. I'm sure that, had we chosen to structure and organise our forest trip in that way, it would have been much shorter, slightly more fraught and would have needed to involve the promise of a reward for good behaviour at the end.

Using Explore Together as a tool to encourage our communities to engage with the Bible provides all of the same experiences as a forest adventure. Everyone involved is in the same place at the same time. The shared experience is the Bible passage: everyone hears the same words, they are introduced to the same scene, context and characters and are given the same open questions to explore. How they then choose to engage with the passage and questions will differ according to their individual personalities, experience and preferences.

Intentional space is created for the community to hear from God and learn from each other as they share their questions, responses and encounters. Every member of the community becomes actively involved in the learning process as they are given the freedom to participate in the way that is most natural for them.

Let's just take a moment to peer through the window of a community church in a small market town to give us an idea of what happens when a community explore together.

Story

The Sunday morning service is about to start. Alice (4) has already arrived with her parents and her little brother Jack (2); they are running about while their mum rehearses with the worship band and their dad sets up chairs. Katie is also there, helping her mum get the cups ready for coffee. Katie (15) has Down syndrome; her ability to communicate verbally is limited and she has the cognitive ability of a 6- to 8-year-old.

Alan (65), a church leader, has arrived early and is positioning himself at the entrance to welcome people as they arrive. He shakes hands with Nigel (30) – this is the first time Nigel has ever been to church; he has a friend who goes to this one and he has decided to come with her. He has been exploring spirituality through Buddhism and Reiki, and is interested in finding out a bit about Christianity.

Today is an Explore Together service; the community will be exploring two Bible passages this morning following the theme of being chosen by God: 1 Samuel 16, the anointing of David, and Mark 3:13–19, Jesus chooses the twelve.

The service starts with a welcome, followed by a short DVD clip, to help the community focus on the wonder of creation and the Creator, and then some sung worship and prayer. The Bible passages are shared creatively, and the historical and geographical context for each passage is explained. Once the passages have been shared the community are invited to think about three questions:

What do these passages tell us about who God is?
What is God saying to you?
What do you want to say to him?

After a prayer everyone is invited to go and explore the Bible passages.

Nigel's experience
Nigel chooses to go to the chat zone where he can discuss the passages with others. He is joined by 15 others including two members of the church leadership team, a retired minister with 40 years' experience of teaching, a mixture of men and women of varying ages and experience, three teenage girls and a few toddlers who have come into the group with their mums.

After reading through the passages again and revisiting the questions, Nigel is able to ask lots of questions that he has about the value of women in the church, commenting on how the Bible seems very male focused. Everyone becomes engaged in the discussion; although the young people in the group don't contribute much verbally they are able to hear authentic questions being asked and witness the interaction between the different members of the group sharing their varying experiences. The opportunity to discuss the passages challenges the more mature Christians in the community to think about their own understanding and to share their wisdom and knowledge.

Nigel's first experience of church forged relationships with others which then led him into a relationship with Jesus. Two years later he was baptised and is now an enthusiastic disciple of Jesus, sharing his new found faith with his friends and family.

Alice's experience
Alice's mum chooses to explore the passages in the colour zone where she reads through them again and begins to think about the questions using coloured chalk on black paper. Alice chooses to do this too, and as they chalk they talk about how being chosen to be a friend of God makes them feel.

Alice stays with her mum for a few minutes and then wanders over to join her dad and little brother in the busy zone. Alice's brother is pressing his fingers into the play dough while her dad and two other men are pushing plastic bricks together as they talk about the questions. Alice hears her dad talking about the Bible with the other men, makes a car with some of the bricks, helps Jack cut heart shapes out of his play dough, puts one of the hearts in her pocket along with the car she has made and skips over to the word zone.

There are a number of people quietly reading and writing there. Alice helps herself to a copy of the story of David the shepherd boy from *The Big Bible Storybook*, and Ella, one of the teenagers in the word zone, reads it with her. Alice asks her what she is writing and Ella explains that she has written a letter to God thanking him for choosing her to be his friend. Alice then picks up a pencil and copies the words, 'David', 'God', 'Alice', 'Mummy', 'Daddy', 'Jack' and 'Ella' onto a sheet of paper. She draws a big heart, folds up the paper and puts it in her pocket. She then goes back to the colour zone where her mum is still drawing with the chalk. She shows her mum what she has done and her mum talks to her about the picture she has drawn.

The time for exploring passes quickly. During this time of exploration Alice has been occupied, safe and welcome, and she and all the other young children have been able to engage at their own level and pace. Although they may not have been able to fully answer the questions, they are very much part of the exploring community.

Katie's experience
Katie loves to paint, and so heads straight for the colour zone where the paint palettes and brushes are waiting. First she paints her name and a house; she then looks at some of the pictures of Jesus and his disciples that are on the wall around the area. She notices a picture of David being anointed by Samuel. She asks a woman standing next to her, 'Who's that?' pointing to David, 'What's that?' The woman answers her questions by telling her a potted version of the stories using the pictures.

Katie then turns her attention to the painting that the woman has done, 'What's that?' The woman explains. Katie then carefully begins to paint a copy of the woman's painting onto a fresh sheet of paper. The woman compliments Katie on her painting skills; Katie smiles, gives the woman a hug and tells her that she loves her. Katie asks the same questions of all of the people who are painting, making her own copies of their art work. Katie stays in the colour zone for the whole time, making friends, asking questions, giving hugs and creating masterpieces. Katie is included in everyone else's activities; she has been able to engage at her own level alongside others of varying ages.

Alan's experience

The quiet zone offers Alan the space he craves to reflect on the Bible passage and to wait on God. He appreciates the knowledge that in this zone no one will interrupt his thoughts or try to talk to him. He shares the space with three other men, a teenage boy and two older women. Alan is interested to see that Josh, the teenage boy, has chosen to come to the quiet zone. He has always found it quite difficult to engage in conversation with Josh and realises that Josh's reluctance to talk might not be teenage angst after all – maybe he is just quiet and reflective.

Alan has to work very hard to engage with people on a one-to-one level; being on the welcome team is his attempt to break out of his comfort zone. Preaching has never been a problem to him but small talk is a huge challenge. Although Alan is retired he is a very busy man, he is on many town committees, involved in the 'Christians Against Poverty' and 'Food Bank' projects, he runs a Bible study group at a local hostel and is a school governor. Today he really appreciates the opportunity to just be quiet and reflect on God's Word.

After 20 minutes of exploring the community is called back and asked to discuss in groups of three to five their responses to the questions. Nigel is happy to share his thoughts with his group and is encouraged and inspired by what the other people in his group have to share.

Alice joins her mum in a group with three other adults and Ella. When given the opportunity to share her response to the question, 'What do you want to say to God?', Ella reads the letter that she had written to God and also helps Alice to tell the group about the story they read together from the children's Bible story book. Alice wants to read the letter she has written, too, so she unfolds it carefully and begins to read, 'Thank you God for Mummy, Daddy, Jack and Ella.' She also adds triumphantly, 'I made a car and a heart.'

Katie is happy to sit with her mum while her group share their responses. She is encouraged by the group to show them 'all' of her paintings.

Alan purposely joins the group that Josh had joined. He shares that he has appreciated the time to just be quiet, speaking a little about the chaos he creates in his life by choosing to follow and serve God. Josh doesn't share anything and there is absolutely no pressure for him to do so. Alan feels that he has got to know Josh a little better that day.

This observation of a typical Explore Together session helps us to underpin the benefits of this method of community Bible engagement. It draws together all of the learning and theory and clearly models how introducing this tool into a community helps that community to grow.

- Explore Together builds community, helping a group to break out of rows, take their focus off one face and voice and enter into Christian dialogue with each other.
- Explore Together encourages participation. Every time a community explores every member is actively involved in the learning process in some way.

- Explore Together involves teenagers, who are able to engage with older and younger generations in productive and encouraging ways. They are given a voice and their contributions are valued. They get to hear authentic stories and have a safe place to ask and explore questions of faith.
- Explore Together manages behaviour as everyone is given a choice. There are no restrictions, which can cause tantrums or irritation, the community are free to choose how they use the time and where they go.
- Explore Together answers questions of culture by creating opportunities to ask those questions in a safe forum. People of all stages and ages in the thinking process are involved in answering them.
- Explore Together frees opinion. The community is encouraged to think about, voice and discuss their own opinion and understanding of the Bible in a healthy and supportive environment.
- Explore Together nourishes authenticity by sharing real stories of faith and life.
- Explore Together recognises the power of the Bible and the Holy Spirit. Space is created for the Bible to be read, explored and shared under the guidance and power of the Holy Spirit.
- Explore Together grows confidence in vocalising faith. Every member is encouraged to share their experience and reflections. A large part of being able to share your faith is having the confidence to talk about it. Explore Together provides opportunities to learn and practise this skill in a safe, loving and non-judgemental environment.

In summary, Explore Together acts as a spiritual thermometer for the faith community. It allows us to identify where each member of the community is on their journey with God. It frees us to journey together, supporting, encouraging and equipping as we go. Natural gifts of the Holy Spirit are revealed through the process of exploring, and those who may need extra support, prayer and encouragement on their journey are easily identifiable.

Reflect

If you would find it helpful, use the following questions and writing spaces to reflect on the ideas in this chapter.

1   Have you ever chosen to listen to someone speak simply because you like them or their style? Have you ever been a sermon critic?

2   'The disciples weren't taught their faith, they caught it.' How do you feel about this statement? Why? How might you encourage those in your church/community to be disciples who catch faith?

3   Are your church services/community gatherings closer to a 'walk in the park' or a 'forest adventure'?

4   Some might argue that a forest adventure is potentially riskier than a walk in the park. In his book *The Growth of Love* Keith White says, '...children must take risks to learn anything; they will bump into things and fall over, they will completely misunderstand and miscalculate. A world purged of all risk and dangers would be so sterile that is would probably prevent children's growth and maturing.'[1] What benefits might intentionally embracing such risks bring to all age groups?

5   What surprises you in the story about a community exploring together? Who do you think learned the most about God? Who do you think engaged the most? How has exploring together helped the community to grow?

6   How could Explore Together help you to identify those in your community in need of extra support, prayer and encouragement?

1 Keith White, *The Growth of Love*, 2008, p164

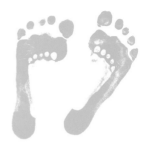

Chapter 5

The practicalities

5

Explore Together is a Bible engagement resource that dispenses with age-centred thinking and focuses on the fact that, even within a group of 20 8-year-olds, a one-size-fits-all approach just won't work well for everyone.

Because the focus is on recognising that whenever a group of people come together there will be diversity, Explore Together can be used as a tool for Bible engagement in any situation. Children's groups, youth groups, house groups, school groups, Bible study groups – anywhere that the Bible is shared is an opportunity to use Explore Together. Its benefits are not restricted to 'All-together' services.

There are six essential steps to an Explore Together session, each of which can be tailored to slot in to any existing structure and space.

For example, Phil uses Explore Together in an all-age service context:

St. Mark's Church
10.30am
All-together service

10.30   Welcome

10.35   Songs

10.40   Prayer

10.45   Notices

10.50   Offering

10.55   Hymn

11.00   Bible Reading: Galatians 5:17–26

11.05   Questions:
What might God want to say to us about the fruit of our lives?
What would you want to say to God?
What one thing do you think God wants you to do after exploring these verses?

11.10   Prayer

11.15   Explore

11.35   Share

11.45   Thank you

11.55   Song

12.00   Final prayer

Before the session, Phil selected the Bible passage for the service he was leading and chose the questions that he wanted the community to explore. He gathered together all the resources he would need for the explore zones (see pages 104 and 105) and was ready to run an all-age service using Explore Together. This is Step 1, which focuses on what needs to be done in advance.

Steps 2 to 6 are shown in bold in the sample service plan and explained in more detail below.

The Explore Together process takes up to 45 minutes in its entirety. It is important that the steps are adhered to and sufficient time is allocated to work through them, as each part of the process is important. If there is no time to 'share', the whole purpose and effectiveness of Explore Together is lost.

Step 1: Prepare

Consider the needs of your community and decide on some open questions

All Scripture is God-breathed and is useful for teaching, rebuking, correcting and training in righteousness, so that the servant of God may be thoroughly equipped for every good work.

2 Timothy 3:16,17

There are many factors that influence the choice we make of Bible passage to form the theme and focus of our services. It may be that the themes are already set through the lectionary or teaching resources. The time of year or occasion, such as Palm Sunday or Pentecost, will draw us automatically to specific parts of the Bible. However we arrive at the choice of passage to explore, we can be confident that it will hold wonders and truths that will deepen our understanding of God.

The Bible has authority and holds the power to challenge, convict and affirm, and what better place to experience this than within a safe community. The core essence of Explore Together is to allow the Bible to speak for itself, which can go against our natural desire to explain its meaning or to wait for someone to explain it to us. It exposes our vulnerability and pushes us out of our comfort zone. Offering the community the opportunity to respond to the Bible passage in their own way will open doors and reveal pathways that will ignite passion, awe and wonder. It requires a huge amount of trust and humility.

As you prepare, study the passage prayerfully and consider the questions you could ask to help the community to focus on the passage and hear God's voice.

Choosing good questions

Asking thought-provoking questions is the key to igniting a vibrant and active Explore Together session. Deciding which questions to use will very much depend on whether a theme is being followed or a particular learning outcome is desired. For example, when exploring the story of Jesus calming the storm the questions chosen could centre around themes of trust, power, faith, obedience or peace, which might look like:

- What does this story tell us about Jesus?
- What storms are raging around you?
- When have you had to trust that Jesus is in control?
- Into which storms does God want you to bring calm?
- How can God use you to bring peace?
- What does this passage teach us about trust, power, faith, obedience or peace?

It may be that the Bible passage chosen doesn't fit into a specific theme. If this is the case, then the questions chosen will need to be more open and less directed, for example:

- What do you think this tells us about God?
- How do you feel after hearing that?
- Why did this happen?
- What does God want to say to you?
- What do you want to say to God?

The purpose of choosing the questions is to provide guidelines that will draw people deeper into the Bible, creating opportunities for exploration, revelation and communion with God and each other. Try not to over complicate the questions and ideally don't ask any more than four questions in a session.

Once the Bible passage and the questions have been selected you are ready to plan and deliver your session.

Step 2: Presenting the Bible

Share the Bible passage and pose the questions
There are so many resources available that help us to present the Bible in thought-provoking ways: drama, film, elaborate prop-filled presentations or just simply reading it out loud. However we choose to present the Word, it is important that we provide a contextual framework. Our understanding of the passage is enhanced when we recognise where it fits within the big story. Bible timelines and maps provide visual references and give the community a secure anchor as they set off to explore just one aspect of the bigger picture. End this part of the session by introducing the questions you have prepared. Don't be tempted to answer them, just plant them gently into their minds.

Step 3: Pray

Commit this time of exploration to God

The purpose of this prayer time is to come before God with expectant and thankful hearts. We bring before God the things that stand in the way of us hearing from him. God wants to communicate with us, but so often there is too much going on in our lives to let us hear. Asking God to open our hearts and minds so that we can hear as we explore the Bible together prepares the community to approach the next step with reverence. This time of prayer can be creative, interactive, responsive, meditative or sung. It could also include communion and intercession.

Ensure that there is a place set aside where people can go if they feel that they need someone to pray with them specifically. Have a small team of people available to offer prayer if required. Prayer ministry should be available throughout an Explore Together session.

Step 4: Explore

Release the community to choose where and how they want to explore the questions

Display the explore questions clearly, taking into consideration the non-readers in your community. Make sure you read out the questions, including simple and more stretching ones. Some may choose to consider all the questions while others may focus on just one. Some may completely ignore the questions and simply open themselves up to God.

Before your session begins you will have prepared and set out six separate and distinct explore zones. These six zones are based on the extensive research carried out into the way people learn, as outlined in Chapter 2, and reflect the way in which we all have different strengths and learning preferences. Each zone is of equal value and importance in the process.

This time of exploring needs to be calm and reverent; playing soft instrumental music in the background while people explore will create an atmosphere conducive to this. Using music that does not invade the thought process helps to keep the focus on the Bible and the questions. If the music used is a recognisable tune people will automatically start to join in or think of the words associated with that song.

It is important to remind the community that this is not a time to catch up with friends or arrange meetings.

Allow the community 15–20 minutes to explore. It is not unusual for people to visit more than one zone, especially those in the community with short attention spans.

In the same way that the background music can invade the thinking process, so can the resources we provide for exploring in the different zones. The intention is to provide resources and materials that will inspire individual creativity and thought. There are no organised crafts in the zones because the focus then becomes the end product and completing the task. By providing only the raw materials the creative process becomes entirely spiritual.

The explore zones

Below are the six different zones with lists of suggested resources. These lists are not exhaustive, they merely offer ideas that can be adapted. All zones need copies of the Explore Together questions.

Colour Zone
This zone will attract those who learn by seeing, image and colour. The colour zone will have several of the following:

- pictures and images depicting the Bible passage displayed around the zone
- paint, paint brushes, crayons, chalk, pastels, marker pens, felt-tip pens
- good quality paper, coloured paper
- flags, ribbons.

Listening Zone
Those who learn by hearing will be attracted by the listening zone. It will usually include:

- MP3 players to listen to the Bible passages and to listen to music
- a sermon could be delivered in this zone.

Chat Zone
The chat zone will attract those who learn by thinking aloud. It will usually have:

- comfortable seating
- an experienced host to lead but not dominate the discussion
- the Bible passage.

Word Zone

Reading and writing are the focus of the word zone. Typical things to include:

- pens, paper, pencils, rulers
- copies of the Bible story for children, Bibles, commentaries, concordances
- selected words from the passage or themes displayed in the zone.

Busy Zone

This zone will attract those who learn by doing. The busy zone should offer a selection of:

- clay, play dough, plastic building bricks, pipe cleaners
- weaving, braiding with coloured threads, string, twine, ribbons, strips of rag
- construction, junk modelling.

Quiet Zone

The quiet zone will attract those who learn by reflecting. It should:

- be a quiet area to simply be with your thoughts and God
- include images
- have the Bible passage.

Step 5: Share

Hear what has been discovered and learn from each other
At the end of the 15 to 20 minute exploring time, indicate to the community that it is time to move into the sharing time.

Encourage the community to come together and share what they have discovered. This is best done in small groups (no fewer than three people and no more than five per group). The sharing time is a valuable time of learning. The community will be supporting, learning from, guiding and encouraging each other. During your sharing time encourage everyone to respect one another, observe appropriate boundaries and follow your church's safeguarding policy.

It is important to remember that very young children are learning through this whole experience. So much about their faith is learnt by watching and hearing the adults in their community talk about God together, and also through the way in which they are treated by the adults in their community. If they are just toddling around or seem distracted or disengaged it does not necessarily mean that they are not learning, joining in or growing in their faith; just smile at them and let them know that they are loved, welcome and very much a part of everything that is taking place.

Step 6: Giving thanks

Give thanks to God for all that he has revealed
This is a drawing together time. It is particularly important at this stage to encourage some of the things that have been shared within the small groups to be presented to the wider community. Offering people the opportunity to feed back allows the whole community to benefit from wider reflections. It can be really exciting and encouraging to hear how God has been communicating.

Whoever is leading this part of the process needs to summarise what has been shared and lead the community into a time of prayer and thanksgiving to God for all that has been revealed.

Gathering a team

Although it is entirely possible to lead an Explore Together session alone, it is much more effective when there is a team of people working together to share the responsibility and to model involvement. Strategically-placed active participants will encourage others to do the same.

The colour, busy and word zones benefit from having a carefully-placed team member present to keep the focus on the questions, to engage in the zone activity and to draw people into the questions without dominating. The chat zone requires an experienced host to keep everyone focused.

The role of a team member
Team members need to:

- Explore alongside the others in the zones.
- Ask questions; we need to model that we never stop asking questions, that we never stop trying to find answers to questions.
- Make discreet notes of helpful and inspiring things that are said in conversation in the zones. (This is particularly helpful when children contribute profound reflections and questions. Quite often a child will forget what they said in the zone when it comes to sharing later. The team member can feed back anything that has been said that may encourage others.)
- Show the same engagement and interest that you would like others to show!
- Support and encourage exploration, ensuring they are half exploring, half supporting.
- Be mindful of those in the zone that may need support, helping them to fully participate in the activity.
- Keep the zone stocked, safe and tidy.

- Consistently and gently draw the focus back to the questions.
- Ask the children in the zones what they are doing and how it is helping them to find answers to the explore questions.
- Not interfere or tell explorers that they are wrong, but feel free to ask more questions to help them think more deeply and to gently challenge their thinking.
- Pray for other explorers while they are exploring, asking God to speak to them clearly.
- Share what they are discovering and explain how they discovered it.

The role of the team during sharing

When everyone comes together in small groups in Step 5, the Explore Together team members should:

- Be actively involved in the small groups.
- If needed, take control of the group, focusing them on sharing their responses to and reflections on the questions.
- Lead from the centre rather than the front, which has a profound impact on how the community engage. Working with a team opens eyes and ears everywhere, allowing the leadership to see and hear how the community are responding to God through his Word, highlighting where extra support and guidance may be needed and identifying gifts that may otherwise be hidden.

The inclusivity of Explore Together

A feeling of belonging is a basic human requirement. However, in many faith communities there are often members who feel or are excluded. More often than not this is a result of programming rather than an intentional effort to create exclusivity. During a service that requires people to sit still and listen, those who physically can't are often encouraged to leave.

I was visiting a church once where a young mother was kindly asked to take her child into the 'cry room'. This was a purpose-built soundproofed room with a big window and speakers. It meant that the mother could sit in there with her little one. The little one could make as much noise as she wanted to and the mother could watch the service through the window and hear what was going on through the speakers. Inclusive?

I once had a conversation with a children's worker who was faced with the prospect of either asking a parent to come into Sunday school with their autistic son or excluding him because he was too disruptive. Inclusive?
I introduced you to Katie in Chapter 4; Katie is now 16 but has the intellectual capabilities of a 7-year-old. She is too old to go to the children's group when they leave the service; they did invite her but she felt out of place because she is a young woman. She can't cope with the discussions and activities of the youth group. Katie doesn't fit neatly into either age group so she stays in the service with her mum, drawing pictures in her note pad while the adults listen to the service. Inclusive?

Exclusivity within the church is often generated by the way we choose to group people. There will always be those who don't fit neatly into the groupings, so whenever we decide to divide our community up into groups it will always exclude someone.

Explore Together models and encourages total inclusivity. Every member of the community can engage at whatever level they are at. If they have a limited concentration span, they can move around at their leisure. Because there are no prescriptive craft activities, which require a particular end product, there are no unrealistic expectations that exclude. Because people are making their own choices about where they go and how they are engaging, behaviour is controlled. Most unacceptable behaviour is a result of boredom or being made to do something. (Please note that I have not confined unacceptable behaviour to children. Adults can behave unacceptably too for exactly the same reasons.) If a member of the community is not able to engage physically or cognitively, there will be many others there to help, support and journey with them.

A community that is truly inclusive provides an environment where every member feels welcome, valued, safe and involved.

Reflect

If you would find it helpful, use the following questions and writing spaces to reflect on the ideas in this chapter.

1   How do you feel about 'allowing the Bible to speak for itself'?

2   Are there people who sometimes feel excluded from your church/community? How could Explore Together help them to engage?

3   Where have you seen 'unacceptable behaviour' in your church/community? What do you think has caused this? How could Explore Together help with this?

4 What could you do to help make your church/community a place where 'every member feels welcome, valued, safe and involved'?

5 Which contexts/groups might you be able to use Explore Together with? (Think outside the box!) Don't forget that Explore Together can be adapted to work in any situation in which you would open the Bible in a group setting.

6 How might you be able to use Explore Together as an outreach tool?

Chapter 6

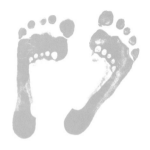

Does Explore Together negate the need for age-specific ministry?

The practice of Explore Together embodies the principle that a multigenerational community can engage with God's Word, learn from each other and grow together.

It is also true that within age-specific ministries there can be diversity of thought, rich experience and God-given creativity for sharing. Explore Together is a rare tool that can be used to nourish all-age community as well as enhance those ministries aimed at specific age groups.

Although some churches do take and use Explore Together as a discrete part of their monthly programme, many churches use it to enrich their existing activities. The beauty of Explore Together is that it can be used within children's groups, youth groups, house groups, school groups, Bible study groups, outreach groups or even within the family home – in fact, anywhere that the Bible is shared. Its benefits are not restricted to all-age services.

We are a very traditional church community. How could Explore Together work within our traditions?

Explore Together embraces tradition but also pushes the boundaries that can be imposed by those traditions. It can fit neatly into the traditional order of things and can also be the catalyst that takes the community on an additional adventure.

Explore Together can be used to help people understand and interpret the meaning and value of symbol and tradition. A whole range of churches from a number of different traditions have taken and used it in different ways. It offers flexibility for churches and communities to make the time of exploring their own, using it so that it fits their group of people.

Our church has many people/a few people. Will it work here?

Over the last five years we have seen Explore Together used in small groups with only a few individuals but also in larger settings. We have known Explore Together to be used within a family home, but also within a programme at Spring Harvest for 450 children.

Key to the smooth running of Explore Together is preparation and planning. It is important to consider how the participants will arrange themselves into small groups. There is a danger that individuals who are close friends, or of similar age and background, will organise themselves into groups, therefore missing out on the excellent opportunity to learn from those who are at a different age or stage in their lives. Inclusivity is key if individuals want to be challenged to learn something new.

While the planning, organisation and setting up of the zones are essential, large or small numbers of people do not present a challenge. No matter how large the group is, Step 5: Sharing is always done in small groups of three to five people. When feeding back in larger churches or groups, having a group of people with roving radio microphones in the congregation works very well.

Isn't Explore Together a bit chaotic, especially with children present?

It is chaotic in the sense that everyone is engaging in different ways, but not because the children are present. The explore zones are designed to embrace a range of learning preferences. Individuals of all ages very quickly find their own preferred activity and become occupied. Although there might be a buzz in the room, activity will be purposeful, colourful and appealing, and everyone has the freedom to move around and make choices in a safe and supportive environment. Many adults find the kinaesthetic dimension of Explore Together appealing too!

Does Explore Together need a lot of space? We have fixed pews in our church building that often restrict what we can do

Explore Together can be planned carefully to fit flexibly into spaces that are different in size and organised in different ways. The explore zones do not all need to happen in one room, they could be spread out to happen in different areas. Your choice of activities can also be tailored to the amount of space you have, and you can creatively use the edges and corners of a room that contains pews. The smallest setting for Explore Together that we have heard about is at a dining room table in a family home.

It sounds a great idea, but I don't really know where to start

The Explore Together website (www.exploretogether.org) provides lots of information.

The *Explore Together Resource Book* gives sessions outlines for twelve sessions, including suggested explore questions and lists of resources required; many of these resources can be downloaded from the website using the access code provided inside the *Resource Book*.

I find sharing my ideas and thoughts very daunting. Do I really have to share my answers? Will others pressure me into talking?

The value of small groups is significant. Individuals have the opportunity to share what they have discovered, and shape the views, thinking and experiences of each other.

It is important that small groups are 'safe places', and that key expectations for how those groups will function are shared. Small groups need to be a place where individuals might not speak. There is huge value in being part of a small group and simply listening. Small groups also need to be a place where people can freely make mistakes, a place where original thoughts and ideas are encouraged. Some individuals might benefit from talking their ideas through one-to-one with another before sharing in a group, but others may never do so.

Individuals within groups need to be careful not to add to pressure others might feel. It should never be an expectation that everyone will talk.

Is Explore Together an alternative to Messy Church?

Messy Church and Explore Together complement each other in many ways. Explore Together can be used as a way of engaging with the Bible within any context. It is just one way of exploring the Bible 'in community'.

Messy Church is a Fresh Expression of church developed to encourage new congregations previously out of reach of 'traditional' church. Rather than replace Messy Church, Explore Together could be used within a Messy Church congregation. In his book *Making Disciples in Messy Church*, Paul Moore mentions that there is a lack of discipleship resources specifically designed for adults and children to use together in an all-age context, like Messy Church, or in the family home.[1] I would strongly suggest that Explore Together ticks that box.

How inclusive is Explore Together for individuals with disabilities and learning difficulties?

Individuals with disabilities and learning difficulties have been involved in Explore Together since its inception. Those with physical difficulties, Down syndrome, diagnoses of ADHD and autistic spectrum conditions have all participated. Individuals are able to express their personal skills, interests and abilities in the explore zone. They can focus on tasks for a length of time that fits their capabilities, and they can share their answers in verbal and nonverbal ways.

It is important to eliminate barriers to participation when planning. For example, if your church or group has members with physical disabilities it is a good idea to ensure that materials and activities are placed at a suitable height. For others, you might wish to use a visual timetable to help an

1 Paul Moore, *Making Disciples in Messy Church*, The Bible Reading Fellowship, 2013, p23

individual know what will be happening next and to show the choices that are available to them in the explore zones.

Explore Together is a scary concept for our church. Is there any way we can implement it in stages?

The key to using Explore Together is to get to know and trust it. Using Explore Together in a smaller group setting to start with helps to build confidence and gets people involved. Using it in a house group setting or with a Sunday school group provides the ideal environment for becoming familiar with the process – children are so much more receptive to new ideas than adults!

I started using Explore Together with a small group of 5 to 11s. Other members of the children's team were involved and experienced first hand its effectiveness. From there we gained the confidence to share what we did in Sunday school with the wider church community. What started for me within a small group of children has now been used with 450 8- to 11-year-olds at Spring Harvest and in large national intergenerational events, too. If you need to, start small but don't be afraid to grow.

How can Explore Together help adults who are reluctant to get out of the pew to engage?

The first thing to establish in situations like this is: Why the reluctance? If the reason concerns mobility and access then measures can be taken to make sure that all areas are easily available or, in extreme cases, the resources can be brought to the person.

More often than not the reluctance comes from the fear of change. The very nature of Explore Together is to provide an environment where every person can engage with the Bible in a way that embraces their natural preferences. There is quite literally something for everyone – the key is making sure that Explore Together is understood before it is forced upon a community that could be less than receptive.

If there are only one or two people for whom change may be difficult, take some time to sit down and explain what you plan to do and why you are doing it. There should be no pressure for people to go to a zone. One of the options is to reflect on the Bible passage quietly, and people could do this by staying in their seats; another is to deliver a sermon in the listening zone.

If the community is filled with people who are reluctant to leave their pews then maybe Explore Together in zone format is not right for you at this time. An alternative option would be to provide a bag (brown paper takeaway bags are ideal) for each person. The bag would contain a small notebook, a pen, a pack of coloured pencils, a small tub of play dough, some images relating to the Bible passage, a copy of the Bible passage or a Bible and a copy of the questions. The process would be the same, except that the community remains seated while they explore. The sharing time would be with those seated around them, and the feedback would happen in the same way as in the original format. This is less than ideal but it could be a stepping stone.

There will need to be a point at which a decision to move forward needs to be taken. Explore Together is a tool created to encourage people to discover the truths of the Bible for themselves. It is another pathway to a deeper relationship with God, intended to help people grow in their faith and reach maturity. Reluctance to engage should be seen as a pastoral opportunity to come alongside that person; to identify barriers and begin to break them down with prayer and persistence. Discipleship is never a done deal, it is a continuous journey that needs to take place in community. It also requires us to address and not ignore telltale signs that indicate the need for intervention – part of being a biblical community is to take that responsibility seriously (Colossians 1:28; Colossians 3:16). Explore Together helps to identify where on that journey we are and where help is needed.

What if someone says something completely off-the-wall?

My immediate response to this question is, 'it's better out than in'. What better place is there to explore your faith and ask your questions than in a community of faith – a community made up of many people with varying levels of understanding, wisdom, knowledge and experience? Explore Together provides a safe environment for people to express their thoughts and ideas, some of which may otherwise never be aired or challenged. The questions help to provide safe boundaries and keep the focus on the desirable aims and outcomes. However, if thoughts or discussions veer off course this should not be perceived as being unhealthy. There are a number of ways in which these diversions and discourses can be embraced and seen as opportunities for growth.

Story

I was once leading an Explore Together session with a group of junior school children. During the group's feedback time one boy shared how he believed that if Jesus were here today he would take a knife and stab all the evil people.

It would have been very easy for me at that point to cut him off and put him right. I could see that there were a number of other children in the group itching to respond, so I just said, 'OK, that's an interesting thought, what does everyone else think?' A girl in the group disagreed. I asked her why she disagreed, her answer went something like this, 'Everything we read in the Bible about Jesus tells us that he loves bad people.

I think if he were here he would talk to them, show them that they are loved, help them to find the right ways to do things like he did with Zacchaeus.'

This led on to a conversation about the things we can do to show love to others. The boy was not humiliated, it was a healthy discussion, managed by an experienced leader in which all the group participated. I asked the boy at the end of the session if he still felt the same. He told me that he understood that Jesus was all about love, but he found it hard to understand why God didn't do something about all the bad people in the world. We then had a brief chat about John 3:16 and why helping people to see how much God loves them through the things we say and do is so important. It was an inspirational conversation that came out of a comment aired in a safe environment.

Earlier in Chapter 5 we looked at the importance of having strategically placed team members who are able to nurture those situations if and when they arise. I introduced you to Nigel in Chapter 4. The questions he had when he went into the chat zone that day led him into a prayer partner relationship with a retired minister and lots of coffee chats with one of the church leaders. Two years later he was baptised.

Bibliography

David Csinos, *Children's Ministry that Fits*, Wipf & Stock, 2011

Neil Fleming, *Teaching & Learning Styles: VARK Strategies*, 2001

James Fowler, *Stages of Faith: The Psychology of Human Development and the Quest for Meaning*, Harper & Row, 1981

Howard Gardner, *Frames of Mind, The Theory of Multiple Intelligences*, Basic Books, 1983

Pauline Hoggarth, *The Seed and the Soil*, Global Christian Library, 2011

Carl Jung, *Psychological Types (Collected Works of CG Jung)*, Routledge, 1992

Marti Olsen Laney, *The Introvert Advantage: How to Thrive in an Extrovert World*, Workman; 2002

Paul Moore, *Making Disciples in Messy Church*, The Bible Reading Fellowship, 2013

Kara Powell and Chap Clark, *Sticky Faith*, Zondervan, 2011

John Westerhoff, *Will Our Children have Faith?*, Moorhouse Publishing, 2012

Keith White, *The Growth of Love*, Barnabas, 2008

Recommended reading

Ivy Beckwith, *Postmodern Children's Ministry: Ministry to Children in the 21st Century Church (Emergent YS)*, Zondervan, 2004

Ivy Beckwith, *Formational Children's Ministry: Shaping Children Using Story, Ritual, and Relationship*, Baker Books, 2010

David Csinos, *Children's Ministry that Fits*, Wipf & Stock, 2011

David Csinos and Ivy Beckwith, *Children's Ministry in the Way of Jesus*, IVP, 2013

Andy Freeman and Pete Greig, *Punk Monk*, Kingsway Publications, 2007

Pauline Hoggarth, *The Seed and the Soil*, Global Christian Library, 2011

Rachel Hunter, *Parenting Children for a Life of Faith*, the Bible Reading Fellowship, 2010

Ronni Lamont, *Understanding Children, Understanding God*, SPCK Publishing, 2007

Rebecca Nye, *Children's Spirituality: What It Is and Why It Matters*, Church House Pubishing, 2009

John Westerhoff, *Will Our Children have Faith?*, Moorhouse Publishing, 2012

Mark Yaconelli, *Contemplative Youth Ministry*, SPCK Publishing, 2006

Explore Together: Resource Book

How do you put the principles of Explore Together into practice?

This fantastic resource book contains 12 Explore Together sessions for you to use in any context, helping groups of any and all ages to engage with the Bible. Topics covered include: salt and light; the birth of Jesus; Easter; Jesus and Nicodemus; God the Creator.

With access to all the multimedia resources you need to run your Explore Together session, this resource offers you a tried and tested method for helping every member of your community to hear from God and learn from each other.

ISBN: 978 1 78506 027 4

RRP: £8.99

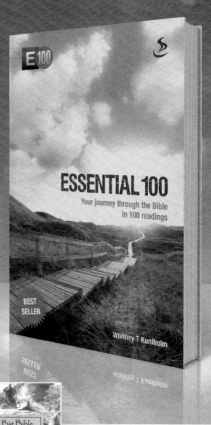

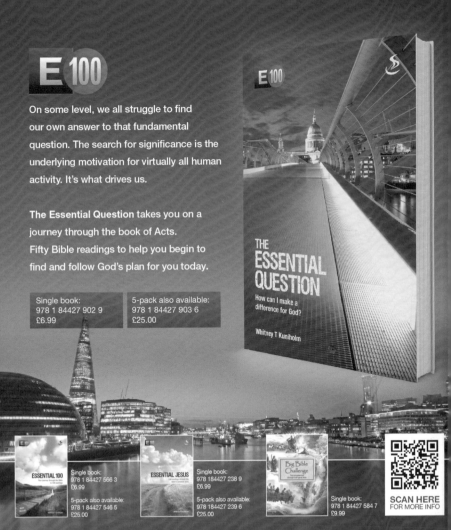